I0006317

Kotlin Development Essentials
Mastering Core Concepts and Techniques

Copyright © 2024 by NOB TREX L.L.C.

All rights reserved. No part of this publication may be reproduced, distributed, or transmitted in any form or by any means, including photocopying, recording, or other electronic or mechanical methods, without the prior written permission of the publisher, except in the case of brief quotations embodied in critical reviews and certain other noncommercial uses permitted by copyright law.

Contents

1 Introduction to Kotlin   11

   1.1 What is Kotlin? 11

   1.2 History of Kotlin 13

   1.3 Kotlin vs. Java: Pros and Cons 15

   1.4 The Kotlin Ecosystem and Community 17

   1.5 Basic Kotlin Program Structure 19

   1.6 Kotlin Tools and IDE Support 21

   1.7 Compiling and Running a Kotlin Program 23

   1.8 Kotlin Applications: From Web to Mobile 25

   1.9 Features of Kotlin 27

   1.10 Advantages of Using Kotlin 30

   1.11 Common Use Cases for Kotlin 32

2 Setting up the Kotlin Development Environment   35

   2.1 Overview of Development Environment Requirements 36

   2.2 Installing the Java Development Kit (JDK) 37

   2.3 Setting Up Kotlin on IntelliJ IDEA 40

   2.4 Setting Up Kotlin on Android Studio 43

2.5   Using Kotlin with Eclipse   46

2.6   Configuring Kotlin in Visual Studio Code   48

2.7   Building and Running Your First Kotlin Application .   50

2.8   Understanding Kotlin Project Structure   52

2.9   Managing Dependencies in Kotlin Projects   54

2.10   Introduction to Gradle for Kotlin   57

2.11   Using the Kotlin Command Line Compiler   59

2.12   Troubleshooting Common Setup Issues   61

3   Kotlin Syntax and Basic Programming Concepts   65

3.1   Understanding Basic Syntax   65

3.2   Declaring Variables and Types   67

3.3   Working with Strings and Characters   69

3.4   Working with Numbers and Arithmetic Operations .   71

3.5   Control Flow: if, when, for, while   74

3.6   Creating and Using Functions   76

3.7   Understanding Nullability and Safe Calls   79

3.8   Using Lambdas and Higher-Order Functions   81

3.9   Introduction to Collections: List, Set, and Map   83

3.10   Basic File I/O in Kotlin   85

3.11   Exception Handling in Kotlin   87

3.12   Annotations and Reflection in Kotlin   89

4   Functions in Kotlin   93

4.1   Defining and Calling Functions   93

4.2   Function Parameters and Return Types   95

4.3   Default and Named Arguments   97

4.4   Using vararg Parameters   99

4.5   Extension Functions and Properties   101

4.6   Higher-Order Functions: Passing Functions as Param-
      eters   103

4.7   Lambda Expressions and Anonymous Functions . . .   105

4.8   Inline Functions and Performance   107

4.9   Tail Recursive Functions   109

4.10 Operator Overloading and Conventions   110

4.11 Infix Notation for Function Calls   113

4.12 Local Functions and Structured Concurrency   115

5   **Working with Collections**   **119**

5.1   Overview of Collections in Kotlin   119

5.2   Creating Lists, Sets, and Maps   121

5.3   Mutable vs Immutable Collections   124

5.4   Accessing Elements in Collections   126

5.5   Collection Operations: Filtering and Mapping   128

5.6   Aggregating Collection Data   130

5.7   Sorting Collections   132

5.8   Sequences and Lazy Evaluation   134

5.9   Using Collection Builders   136

5.10 Working with Ranges and Progressions   138

5.11 Introduction to Kotlin's Collection APIs   140

5.12 Best Practices for Using Collections   142

6   **Object-Oriented Programming in Kotlin**   **145**

6.1   Introduction to OOP Principles in Kotlin   145

6.2   Defining Classes and Creating Objects   147

6.3   Constructor and Initialization Blocks   150

6.4   Properties and Fields: Getters and Setters   152

6.5   Inheritance in Kotlin: Overriding Methods and Prop-
       erties   154

6.6   Abstract Classes and Interfaces   156

6.7   Visibility Modifiers: Public, Private, Protected, and In-
       ternal   158

6.8   Data Classes and Destructuring Declarations   160

6.9   Object Expressions and Declarations: Anonymous
       and Companion Objects   162

6.10   Extension Functions/Properties for Classes   164

6.11   Sealed Classes and Enum Classes   166

6.12   Delegation: By Lazy and By Delegated Properties . .   168

7   **Exploring   Kotlin   Coroutines   for   Asynchronous
    Programming**   **173**

7.1   Introduction to Asynchronous Programming   174

7.2   Understanding Coroutines in Kotlin   175

7.3   Setting up the Coroutine Environment   178

7.4   Basic Coroutine Builders: launch and async   180

7.5   Structured Concurrency and Coroutine Scope   182

7.6   Suspending Functions: The Basics   185

7.7   Coroutine Context and Dispatchers   187

7.8   Combining Coroutines: Sequential and Parallel
       Execution   190

7.9   Error Handling in Coroutines   192

7.10   Flow: Handling Streams of Data   194

7.11   Cancellation and Timeouts in Coroutines   196

7.12   Advanced Coroutine Use Cases and Patterns   199

8 Interoperability with Java **203**

8.1 Introduction to Kotlin-Java Interoperability 203

8.2 Calling Java from Kotlin 206

8.3 Calling Kotlin from Java 208

8.4 Handling Nullability in Kotlin and Java 211

8.5 Using Java Collections in Kotlin 213

8.6 Java Generics and Kotlin Type Parameters 215

8.7 Interoperable Naming: @JvmName Annotation . . . 218

8.8 Creating Kotlin Extensions for Java Classes 219

8.9 Working with Kotlin and Java Annotations 221

8.10 Interoperability Best Practices 224

8.11 Practical Examples of Kotlin-Java Interoperation . . . 226

8.12 Common Pitfalls and How to Avoid Them 229

9 Data Management with Kotlin **233**

9.1 Introduction to Data Management in Kotlin 233

9.2 Working with JSON in Kotlin 235

9.3 Handling XML Data 238

9.4 Using SQLite for Local Data Storage 241

9.5 Exploring Room Database with Kotlin 243

9.6 Kotlin and Firebase for Online Data Management . . 245

9.7 Implementing Data Caching Strategies 248

9.8 Managing Files and Directories in Kotlin 250

9.9 Using Kotlin for Data Serialization and Deserialization 252

9.10 Data Validation and Error Handling 255

9.11 Best Practices for Data Management 258

9.12 Exploring Third-party Libraries for Data Management 261

10 Building Android Apps with Kotlin   **265**

  10.1 Getting Started with Android Development in Kotlin   266

  10.2 Setting Up Your Android Development Environment   268

  10.3 Creating Your First Android App with Kotlin   270

  10.4 Understanding Android Architecture and Lifecycle .   273

  10.5 Designing User Interfaces with XML and Kotlin   . . .   276

  10.6 Handling User Interaction and Events   279

  10.7 Working with Android Layouts and Material Design   282

  10.8 Implementing Navigation and Multi-Screen Apps . .   284

  10.9 Data Persistence: Room, Preferences, and Files 286

  10.10Building Dynamic Applications with LiveData and
       ViewModel   288

  10.11Utilizing Android Networking Libraries with Kotlin .   290

  10.12Adding Multimedia and Camera Features   293

  10.13Publishing Your Android App   296

Preface

"Kotlin Development Essentials: Mastering Core Concepts and Techniques" is meticulously crafted to be an indispensable resource for those eager to explore Kotlin comprehensively, from fundamental principles to advanced application in real-world scenarios. As a progressive language that operates seamlessly on the Java Virtual Machine (JVM), Kotlin has swiftly gained prominence, particularly in Android app development and modern server-side solutions. Its succinct syntax, compatibility with existing Java code, and robust support for functional and concurrent programming paradigms make it an essential toolkit for today's developers.

The principal aim of this text is to build a robust foundation for readers in Kotlin programming, ensuring fluency in core language constructs while delving into its versatile applications. The journey begins with essential setups like configuring the development environment and parsing the unique syntax of Kotlin. It then transitions through layers of complexity, encompassing object-oriented design principles, coroutine-based asynchronous programming, and interfacing with Android development frameworks. This structured approach guarantees a coherent evolution of knowledge, providing smooth passage for novices while presenting layered insights for seasoned programmers.

Each chapter is thoughtfully structured to cover critical components of Kotlin development, replete with examples that vividly illustrate the theory in practice. Readers will glean a holistic understanding of

Kotlin's flexibility and its capacity to drive mobile and desktop development. The volume is replete with practical exercises, meticulously crafted to entrench comprehension through application, propelling students beyond theoretical learning to pragmatic proficiency.

The intended readership is diverse, encompassing individuals from absolute beginners aiming to master Kotlin as their inaugural programming language, to experienced Java developers transitioning into Kotlin's ecosystem, and expert software architects looking to diversify their programming repertoire. Whether your ambition is to engineer cutting-edge Android applications, architect innovative server-side solutions, or simply acquaint yourself with a modern, dynamic programming language, this compendium provides the insights and acumen necessary to attain your objectives.

In the formulation of this book, emphasis is placed not just on language acquisition, but on embedding best practices and fostering a profound grasp of Kotlin's capacity to drive effective and efficient solutions. By journey's end, readers will find themselves poised to address complex programming challenges with Kotlin, empowered with a comprehensive toolkit and a keen understanding of its nuanced, yet robust capabilities.

Chapter 1

Introduction to Kotlin

Kotlin is a statically typed programming language that targets the Java Virtual Machine (JVM), JavaScript, and Native. It is developed by JetBrains and has been gaining popularity for its concise syntax, safety features, and interoperability with Java. Kotlin is officially supported by Google for mobile development on Android, and its adoption has been growing for server-side development, desktop applications, and web development. This chapter provides an overview of Kotlin, including its history, key features, and its burgeoning ecosystem, setting the stage for a deeper dive into the language's syntax and capabilities throughout this guidebook.

1.1 What is Kotlin?

Kotlin is a modern programming language that offers a blend of functional and object-oriented programming paradigms. It is statically typed, which means that the types of variables are known at compile time, enhancing the language's performance and reliability. Kotlin's primary design goal was to create a language that is concise, expressive, and safe. This is achieved through various language features that reduce boilerplate code, prevent common programming errors, and ensure null safety.

One of the distinctive characteristics of Kotlin is its interoperability with Java. Kotlin code can seamlessly call Java code, and Java code can call Kotlin code. This interoperability is facilitated by Kotlin's targeting of the Java Virtual Machine (JVM) as one of its primary platforms. Additionally, Kotlin can be compiled to JavaScript, allowing its use in frontend web development, and to native binaries, which makes it applicable for developing on platforms where JVM is not an option.

The syntax of Kotlin is designed to be intuitive and familiar to those already acquainted with Java. However, it introduces several improvements and new features that streamline development. For example, Kotlin removes the need for semicolons at the end of each statement, supports type inference which allows the compiler to deduce the type of a variable from its initializer, and introduces concise syntax for functions and variable declarations.

Following is an example of a simple Kotlin program that prints "Hello, World!" to the standard output:

```
1  fun main(args: Array<String>) {
2      println("Hello, World!")
3  }
```

In this example, fun keyword is used to declare a function. The function named main is the entry point of a Kotlin application. The println function is used to print a line to the console, and it is part of Kotlin's standard library. This simple example underscores Kotlin's simplicity and how it aims to reduce verbosity without sacrificing readability or functionality.

Kotlin's safety features include null safety, which helps in reducing the risk of null pointer exceptions, a common source of runtime errors in many programming languages. Kotlin achieves this through its nullable and non-nullable type system, where every variable must be explicitly marked as nullable or not.

Consider the following code snippet demonstrating Kotlin's null safety:

```
1  var a: String = "abc"
```

```
2   //a = null // Compilation error
3
4   var b: String? = "abc"
5   b = null // Allowed
```

In this example, variable a is of type String, which cannot hold a null value, and attempting to assign null to it will result in a compilation error. On the other hand, variable b is of type String?, a nullable string type, which can hold a null value.

Kotlin's approach to null safety and its concise and expressive syntax make it a compelling choice for modern application development, offering developers the tools to write safe, readable, and concise code.

1.2 History of Kotlin

Kotlin, a statically typed programming language, was conceived by JetBrains, a software development company known for creating IntelliJ IDEA, an integrated development environment (IDE) for Java programming. The primary motivation behind the development of Kotlin was to address the limitations and issues encountered by Jet-Brains developers with Java, particularly concerning verbosity, null safety, and the absence of functional programming features. Kotlin was designed to be fully interoperable with Java, thereby enabling developers to utilize existing Java libraries and frameworks while offering an improved syntax and features set.

The development of Kotlin began in 2010, with JetBrains aiming to create a language that would run on the Java Virtual Machine (JVM) and could compile as fast as Java. Kotlin's name is derived from Kotlin Island, located near St. Petersburg, Russia, where one of JetBrains' development teams was based. The choice of naming the language after a geographical location follows a tradition seen in other programming languages, such as Java named after the Indonesian island.

Kotlin was officially released as an open-source project in February 2012 under the Apache 2 license. The initial version, Kotlin v0.1, was described as a new language for the JVM capable of leveraging existing Java libraries and frameworks while offering additional features to enhance developer productivity and application performance.

Significant milestones in Kotlin's history include:

- In July 2011, Kotlin was announced to the public for the first time, indicating JetBrains' commitment to developing a modern language for JVM and Android.

- The release of Kotlin v1.0 in February 2016 marked the language's official stability, ensuring backward compatibility for future versions and signalling readiness for production use.

- At the Google I/O conference in May 2017, Google announced first-class support for Kotlin on Android. This endorsement significantly boosted Kotlin's popularity among mobile developers, leading to widespread adoption for Android application development.

- Kotlin/Native, introduced in April 2017 as a technology preview, enabled Kotlin code compilation into native binaries for various platforms, including iOS, macOS, Linux, and Windows, highlighting the language's versatility beyond the JVM.

- In May 2019, Kotlin was announced by Google as its preferred language for Android app development, further solidifying Kotlin's position in the mobile development ecosystem.

- Kotlin 1.3, released in October 2018, introduced coroutines for asynchronous programming, a feature that significantly simplified coding for complex asynchronous tasks such as network IO and concurrency.

- Kotlin 1.4, released in August 2020, focused on improving the performance and tooling support, cementing its place as a modern, efficient language for various types of software development projects.

14

Throughout its development, Kotlin has been guided by principles aimed at improving coding efficiency and safety. The language's type system is designed to eliminate the dreaded NullPointerException, a common source of runtime errors in Java. Moreover, Kotlin introduces several modern features such as extension functions, higher-order functions, and data classes, fostering a more expressive and concise codebase.

The language's philosophy emphasizes pragmatism and interoperability, striving to make Kotlin not just an alternative to Java but a superior choice for modern software development needs, without forcing developers to abandon the Java ecosystem.

With its comprehensive tooling support, IntelliJ IDEA integration, and seamless interoperability with Java, Kotlin has managed to carve out a significant niche for itself in the software development world, gaining traction across web, mobile, desktop, and server-side development. Its evolution reflects JetBrains' commitment to addressing real-world development challenges, offering a potent combination of modern features, performance, and safety.

1.3   Kotlin vs. Java: Pros and Cons

In this section, we will discuss the advantages and disadvantages of Kotlin compared to Java. This comparison is critical for understanding why Kotlin might be the preferred choice in certain scenarios and why Java continues to hold its ground in others.

- **Syntax and Conciseness:** Kotlin offers a more concise and expressive syntax compared to Java. This results in fewer lines of code for the same functionality, which can lead to fewer bugs and easier maintenance. For example, Kotlin eliminates the need for semicolons at the end of each statement and introduces a range of features such as higher-order functions, extension functions, and smart casts that simplify the coding process.

```
1     // Kotlin
```

```
2    fun sum(a: Int, b: Int) = a + b
3
4    // Java
5    public int sum(int a, int b) {
6        return a + b;
7    }
```

- **Null Safety:** One of Kotlin's major advantages over Java is its built-in null safety feature. Kotlin's type system is designed to eliminate the dread NullPointerException from code, by incorporating inherent null checks during compile time. Java, on the other hand, requires explicit null checks to avoid runtime exceptions.

```
1    // Kotlin
2    var name: String? = null // Nullable type
3    println(name?.length) // Safe call
4
5    // Java
6    String name = null;
7    if (name != null) {
8        System.out.println(name.length());
9    } else {
10       System.out.println("name is null");
11   }
```

- **Extension Functions:** Kotlin allows developers to extend existing classes with new functionality without having to inherit from the class— a feature not available in Java. Extension functions facilitate cleaner and more readable code.

```
1    // Kotlin extension function
2    fun String.countWords(): Int = split(" ").size
3    println("Hello World".countWords()) // Outputs 2
4
5    // Java equivalent would require a utility class
6    public class StringUtils {
7        public static int countWords(String s) {
8            return s.split(" ").length;
9        }
10   }
11   println(StringUtils.countWords("Hello World")); // Outputs 2
```

- **Coroutines for Asynchronous Programming:** Kotlin has first-class support for coroutines, which facilitate asynchronous programming in a more efficient and straightforward way compared to Java's verbose

CompletableFuture or threads. Coroutines allow easy creation of non-blocking or asynchronous code, which is especially beneficial in environments with limited resources, such as Android.

- **Interoperability with Java:** Kotlin is fully interoperable with Java, meaning that it can use all existing Java libraries, JVM, and frameworks, which makes transitioning from Java to Kotlin smooth and gradual. Java, however, cannot directly use Kotlin's extended features.

- **Compilation Speed:** While Kotlin introduces several improvements over Java, it also comes with a generally slower compilation speed. The additional overhead during compilation might affect large projects where build times are critical.

- **Learning Curve:** For developers experienced in Java, learning Kotlin is relatively straightforward due to its similar structure and interoperability. However, Kotlin's unique features and syntactic sugar do have an associated learning curve. Newcomers might find Kotlin's concise syntax and plethora of features overwhelming at first.

Considering the points mentioned above, the choice between Kotlin and Java depends on the specific requirements of the project, the team's familiarity with the languages, and the anticipated future direction of the application. Kotlin offers modern features and a more expressive syntax, making it a compelling choice for new projects, whereas Java's vast ecosystem and robustness continue to make it suitable for a wide range of applications.

1.4 The Kotlin Ecosystem and Community

The Kotlin ecosystem encompasses a wide array of libraries, tools, frameworks, and plugins specifically designed to enhance the Kotlin development experience. These resources are integral to the language's adoption and its capability to deliver high-quality software applications across different platforms. The Kotlin community, composed of developers, contributors, and enthusiasts, plays a pivotal role in the ecosystem's growth, offering support, creating resources, and driving the evolution of the language.

Major Components of the Kotlin Ecosystem

- **Libraries and Frameworks:** Kotlin boasts a rich collection of libraries and frameworks that simplify various aspects of application development. For instance, Ktor is a framework for building asynchronous servers and clients in connected systems. Similarly, Arrow is a comprehensive library that augments Kotlin's functional programming capabilities.

- **Tools:** The Kotlin ecosystem is supported by an array of powerful tools that streamline the development process. These include the Kotlin compiler itself, which is capable of targeting the JVM, JavaScript, and Native platforms. The Kotlin Plugin for IntelliJ IDEA and Android Studio facilitates Kotlin development with features like code completion, refactorings, and debugging.

- **Integration and Interoperability Tools:** Kerning is essential in the Kotlin ecosystem, enabling seamless interoperability with Java, Android, and other languages. This is facilitated by tools and features like the Java-to-Kotlin converter, which helps developers transition their existing Java codebase to Kotlin efficiently.

The Kotlin Community

The Kotlin community is a vibrant and rapidly growing group of individuals passionate about Kotlin and its advancement. The community's contributions are manifold and include:

- **Open Source Contributions:** Many Kotlin libraries and tools are open-source, inviting contributions from the global developer community. This collaborative effort ensures continuous improvement and innovation within the ecosystem.

- **Knowledge Sharing:** Developers share their expertise and insights through blog posts, tutorials, webinars, and conference presentations. This wealth of shared knowledge promotes best practices and enables newcomers to get up to speed quickly.

- **Community Support:** Kotlin's official forum, Slack channels, and Stack Overflow tags provide platforms for developers to seek help, exchange ideas, and collaborate on projects. This strong peer support network is a cornerstone of Kotlin's welcoming and inclusive community.

The Kotlin ecosystem and community collectively foster an environment conducive to learning, innovation, and collaboration. As Kotlin continues to evolve and expand its reach, the synergy between its technical capabilities and the vibrant community is a key driver behind the language's growing popularity and adoption.

1.5   Basic Kotlin Program Structure

Kotlin programs follow a concise and structured format that is both easy for beginners to learn and powerful enough for experts to exploit efficiently. Understanding the foundational structure of a Kotlin program is essential for writing effective Kotlin code. This section discusses the key elements that constitute the basic structure of a Kotlin program, including the main function, declarations of variables and functions, and comments.

Firstly, every Kotlin program must contain an entry point, which is the main function where the program starts its execution. This function is declared using the `fun` keyword followed by the name `main` and a pair of parentheses. If a program takes command-line arguments, the `main` function includes a parameter for an array of strings (`Array<String>`). Here is an example of the simplest form of a Kotlin program with the main function:

```
1  fun main() {
2      println("Hello, Kotlin!")
3  }
```

In this example, the println function is used to output the string "Hello, Kotlin!" to the console. The program begins execution within the main function and terminates once the end of the function is reached.

Variables in Kotlin are declared using the var and val keywords for mutable and immutable variables, respectively. Kotlin requires explicit type specification only when it cannot infer the type. Here is an illustration of variable declarations:

```
1  val name: String = "JetBrains"
2  var version: Int = 1
```

In this code snippet, name is a constant (immutable variable) of type String, and version is a mutable variable of type Int. Kotlin enforces type safety, meaning that a variable cannot be reassigned to a value of a different type once it is declared.

Functions in Kotlin are defined using the fun keyword, followed by the function name, parameter list in parentheses, and the return type. If a function does not return any value, the return type is Unit, which can be omitted. Here is an example of a simple function declaration:

```
1  fun greet(name: String): Unit {
2      println("Hello, $name")
3  }
```

This function, greet, takes one parameter of type String and prints a greeting to the console. The $ symbol is used to reference variables within strings, known as string templates.

Lastly, comments in Kotlin can be added using two forward slashes (//) for single-line comments or a block delimited by /* and */ for multi-line comments. Here is an example demonstrating both:

```
1  // This is a single-line comment
2
3  /*
4  This is a multi-line comment
5  that spans multiple lines.
```

```
6  */
```

Comments are ignored by the compiler and serve as notes or explanations for the code, making it easier to understand and maintain.

In summary, the basic structure of a Kotlin program includes the `main`
function, variable declarations, function definitions, and comments.
Mastery of these elements provides a solid foundation for delving
deeper into Kotlin's features and capabilities.

1.6   Kotlin Tools and IDE Support

Kotlin, while a relatively new entrant in the programming world,
has rapidly gained support from a wide array of development tools
and integrated development environments (IDEs). This widespread
support is instrumental in providing a seamless development
experience, which is crucial for both beginners and experienced
developers alike.   The primary tools and IDEs that significantly
enhance Kotlin development are discussed in detail in this section.

Firstly, JetBrains IntelliJ IDEA stands out as the leading IDE for Kotlin
development. IntelliJ IDEA comes in two editions: Community and
Ultimate. The Community edition is free and provides basic features
sufficient for Kotlin development, including:

- Syntax highlighting

- Code auto-completion

- Debugging support

- Unit testing

- Version control

The Ultimate edition, on the other hand, is paid and includes
advanced features such as database tools, web development
support, and mobile development with Kotlin Multiplatform. The

tight integration of Kotlin in IntelliJ IDEA is not surprising, given that both the language and the IDE are developed by JetBrains. This integration ensures that developers benefit from the latest features and improvements in Kotlin.

Another notable IDE is Android Studio, which is based on IntelliJ IDEA. Given Kotlin's official support for Android development, Android Studio provides comprehensive tools for building Android apps with Kotlin, including:

- Kotlin-specific refactoring and lint checks

- First-class support for Kotlin coroutines

- Integration with Kotlin build tools

For those who prefer lightweight editors over full-fledged IDEs, Visual Studio Code (VS Code) offers substantial support for Kotlin through extensions. The most popular Kotlin extension for VS Code features include syntax highlighting, code snippets, and debugging. While not as deeply integrated as IntelliJ IDEA or Android Studio, VS Code is an excellent option for developers who enjoy its flexibility and wide range of supported programming languages.

In terms of build systems and project management, Gradle and Maven are the two most widely used tools in Kotlin projects. Gradle, in particular, has first-class support for Kotlin through the Kotlin DSL, allowing build scripts to be written in Kotlin itself. This feature not only makes the build scripts more comprehensible for Kotlin developers but also benefits from the type safety and expressiveness of the language.

Finally, the Kotlin compiler itself is a critical tool in the Kotlin ecosystem. It can be used directly through the command line for compiling Kotlin code into bytecode for the JVM, JavaScript, or native binaries. The compiler options enable developers to target different platforms and optimize their Kotlin applications accordingly.

The Kotlin ecosystem is well-supported by a range of tools and IDEs that cater to various preferences and project requirements. The synergy between these tools and Kotlin's language features makes Kotlin development efficient, enjoyable, and productive.

1.7 Compiling and Running a Kotlin Program

Compiling and running a Kotlin program involves a series of steps that are straightforward but essential for the successful execution of any Kotlin code. The process can broadly be divided into two main phases: compilation and execution. First, the Kotlin compiler converts the source code into bytecode, which is a set of instructions that the Java Virtual Machine (JVM) can understand. Then, the JVM executes this bytecode to run the program. Let's delve deeper into each of these steps to understand how to compile and run a Kotlin program efficiently.

Compilation

The Kotlin compiler plays a crucial role in the development cycle. It takes Kotlin source files, with the extension .kt, and compiles them into a format that can be executed by the JVM or another target platform. For JVM-based applications, the output is bytecode contained in .class files. For JavaScript or Native targets, the output varies to fit the execution environment.

To compile a Kotlin program for the JVM, you can use the command-line tool provided by the Kotlin distribution. The basic syntax for compiling a Kotlin file named Main.kt is as follows:

```
1   kotlinc Main.kt -include-runtime -d Main.jar
```

This command tells the Kotlin compiler (kotlinc) to compile the file Main.kt, include the Kotlin runtime in the resulting JAR file (-include-runtime), and name the output JAR file Main.jar (-d Main.jar). The inclusion of the runtime is necessary for the JAR file to be executed independently on any JVM without needing to install Kotlin.

Execution

Once a Kotlin program has been successfully compiled into a JAR file, it can be executed on the JVM using the java command. The syntax for executing a JAR file named Main.jar is as follows:

```
1   java -jar Main.jar
```

This command invokes the JVM to execute the compiled Kotlin program contained in the Main.jar file. If the program is designed to output text, the command prompt will display this output upon successful execution.

Using Kotlin with IDEs

For many developers, working within an Integrated Development Environment (IDE) significantly enhances productivity. Popular IDEs such as IntelliJ IDEA, which is developed by JetBrains (the creators of Kotlin), and Android Studio provide extensive support for Kotlin.

When using an IDE, the process of compiling and running Kotlin programs is streamlined. Most IDEs feature built-in tools to automate and manage the compilation process, often only requiring a simple button press or keyboard shortcut to build and run the project. For instance, in IntelliJ IDEA, running a Kotlin program typically involves selecting the green arrow button next to the main function or pressing Shift+F10.

In summary, compiling and running a Kotlin program involves compiling the Kotlin source code to bytecode with the kotlinc command-line tool, then executing the resulting bytecode on the JVM with the java command. Utilizing IDEs can simplify these processes through automation and graphical interfaces. Understanding these steps is crucial for every Kotlin developer, from beginners writing their first program to seasoned professionals developing complex applications.

1.8 Kotlin Applications: From Web to Mobile

Kotlin's versatility as a programming language is evident in its widespread application across various development domains. From web development to mobile app creation, Kotlin's features such as concise syntax, safety, and interoperability with Java have made it an attractive option for developers.

Web Development with Kotlin

Kotlin's adoption for server-side and web development has been facilitated by frameworks such as Ktor and Spring Boot. Ktor, a framework developed by JetBrains, leverages Kotlin's coroutines for handling asynchronous operations efficiently, thus offering a robust foundation for creating server-side applications.

Consider the following example of a simple HTTP server using Ktor:

```
import io.ktor.server.engine.*
import io.ktor.server.netty.*
import io.ktor.server.routing.*
import io.ktor.server.application.*
import io.ktor.server.response.*

fun main() {
    embeddedServer(Netty, port = 8080) {
        routing {
            get("/") {
                call.respondText("Hello, Kotlin Web!")
            }
        }
    }.start(wait = true)
}
```

This snippet showcases the simplicity and expressiveness of Kotlin for web development. The server runs on port 8080 and responds with "Hello, Kotlin Web!" to GET requests to the root URL.

Mobile Development with Kotlin

Kotlin's most significant stride in mobile development came when Google announced it as a preferred language for Android app development. Kotlin brings several advantages to Android development, including null safety, extension functions, and concise syntax, which significantly enhance the development experience and reduce the likelihood of bugs.

An example of a simple Android application written in Kotlin is shown below:

```
import android.os.Bundle
import androidx.appcompat.app.AppCompatActivity
import android.widget.TextView

class MainActivity : AppCompatActivity() {
    override fun onCreate(savedInstanceState: Bundle?) {
        super.onCreate(savedInstanceState)
        setContentView(R.layout.activity_main)

        val textView = findViewById<TextView>(R.id.text_view)
        textView.text = "Hello, Kotlin Android!"
    }
}
```

This code outlines the structure of a basic Android activity that sets the content view from a layout resource and updates a TextView to display "Hello, Kotlin Android!". It demonstrates Kotlin's seamless integration with the Android SDK, enabling developers to write more concise and readable code compared to Java.

Desktop and Native Applications

Beyond web and mobile, Kotlin is also making inroads into desktop application development through TornadoFX, a lightweight JavaFX framework for Kotlin. Additionally, Kotlin/Native facilitates the creation of native applications for platforms like iOS, macOS, Windows, and Linux, by compiling Kotlin code to native binaries.

This versatility across platforms underscores Kotlin's flexibility and its potential to become a unifying language for developing applications across the spectrum, from web to mobile and even desktop environments.

Kotlin's applicability spans web, mobile, and desktop development, propelled by its concise syntax, safety features, and the robust support from its ecosystem. Its interoperability with existing Java codebases and tools ensures a smooth transition for developers looking to adopt Kotlin for their projects. As the Kotlin community grows and evolves, it is expected to see further expansion of Kotlin's applications and its adoption across more platforms and development contexts.

1.9 Features of Kotlin

Kotlin is distinguished by a set of powerful features that contribute to its growing popularity among developers, particularly for Android application development, web applications, and server-side programming. This section will discuss Kotlin's most notable features, including its concise syntax, null safety, extension functions, higher-order functions and lambdas, smart casts, type inference, and coroutines for asynchronous programming.

Concise Syntax

The concise syntax of Kotlin is one of its most celebrated features. It significantly reduces the amount of boilerplate code that developers need to write compared to Java. For example, data classes in Kotlin automatically generate equals(), hashCode(), toString(), and copy() functions, which need to be manually implemented in Java.

```
1   data class User(val name: String, val age: Int)
```

Comparatively, the equivalent Java class would require substantially more lines of code to achieve the same functionality.

Null Safety

Kotlin's type system is designed to eliminate the NullPointerException from the code. It distinguishes between nullable and non-nullable references.

```
1  var a: String = "abc"
2  // 'a' cannot be null
3
4  var b: String? = "abc"
5  // 'b' can be set to null
6  b = null // ok
```

This distinction helps in catching null pointer errors at compile time rather than at runtime.

Extension Functions

Kotlin allows developers to extend a class with new functionality without inheriting from the class. This is done via extension functions which are a powerful feature for adding methods to classes without modifying their source code.

```
1  fun String.addExclamation(): String {
2      return this + "!"
3  }
4
5  println("Hello".addExclamation()) // Output: Hello!
```

Higher-Order Functions and Lambdas

Kotlin treats functions as first-class citizens, allowing them to be stored in variables and data structures, passed as arguments to other functions, and returned from functions.

```
1  val sum: (Int, Int) -> Int = { x, y -> x + y }
2  println(sum(2, 3)) // Output: 5
```

Lambdas in Kotlin are a simple way to create function literals on the fly.

Smart Casts

The smart cast feature of Kotlin automatically casts types if they have been checked in a control structure. This eliminates the need for explicit casting, making the code cleaner and more readable.

```
1  fun demo(x: Any) {
2      if (x is String) {
3          println(x.length) // x is automatically cast to String
4      }
5  }
```

Type Inference

Kotlin is able to infer the type of variables and expressions if they are not explicitly declared, reducing redundancy and verbosity in the code.

```
1  val a = "abc" // The type String is inferred
```

Coroutines for Asynchronous Programming

Coroutines are a standout feature of Kotlin, offering a powerful and efficient way to handle asynchronous programming. Coroutines simplify the execution of asynchronous operations, such as network calls or database transactions, by writing code in a sequential manner.

```
1  suspend fun loadData(): Data {
2      // expensive operation
3  }
```

Kotlin's coroutines are integrated into the language's type system, which allows for safe and concise code that is easy to understand and maintain.

The combination of these features makes Kotlin a particularly effective language for modern application development. Its comprehensive range of functionalities caters to a variety of programming paradigms and application scenarios, from mobile and web application development to server-side systems.

1.10   Advantages of Using Kotlin

Kotlin offers a multitude of benefits that collectively contribute to
its growing adoption and popularity among developers, especially
those working in Android mobile development. The advantages of
using Kotlin can be attributed to its design, which emphasizes
safety, conciseness, and interoperability. Below, we meticulously
detail these advantages to provide a comprehensive understanding.

- **Conciseness**: Kotlin's syntax is designed to reduce the amount
  of boilerplate code, which is common in Java. This conciseness
  not only makes the code more readable but also less prone to errors. For example, consider the implementation of a data class
  in Java versus Kotlin:

```
1    // Java
2    public class User {
3        private String name;
4        private int age;
5
6        public User(String name, int age) {
7            this.name = name;
8            this.age = age;
9        }
10
11       // Getters and Setters
12   }
13
14   // Kotlin
15   data class User(val name: String, val age: Int)
```

  The Kotlin version succinctly provides the same functionality
  with less code, thanks to the `data` keyword, which
  automatically generates necessary functions such as `equals()`,
  `hashCode()`, and `toString()`.

- **Safety Features**: The language's type system is designed to
  eliminate NullPointerExceptions (NPEs), known as the Billion
  Dollar Mistake. This is achieved through its null safety
  feature.

```
1    var a: String = "abc"
2    //a = null // Compilation error
3
4    var b: String? = "abc"
5    b = null // Allowed
```

In the above example, variable a can not be set to null, ensuring safety against NPE, while variable b, explicitly declared as nullable with ?, can hold a null value.

- **Interoperability with Java**: One of Kotlin's most valuable features is its seamless interoperability with Java. Kotlin code can be mixed with Java code, allowing developers to use all existing Java libraries, frameworks, and tools. This feature mitigates the risk of adopting Kotlin in existing Java projects and enables gradual migration.

```
1    // Calling Java code from Kotlin
2    Date date = new Date()
3    String formatted = SimpleDateFormat("dd/MM/yyyy").format(date)
4    println(formatted)
```

- **Coroutines Support**: Kotlin introduces coroutines as a core feature, enabling asynchronous programming patterns in a more concise and straightforward manner. Coroutines facilitate writing non-blocking code, which is crucial for applications that require high levels of responsiveness and scalability.

- **Extension Functions**: Kotlin allows developers to extend a class with new functionality without inheriting from the class with extension functions. This feature enables a more idiomatic way to add functionality to classes.

```
1    fun String.lastChar(): Char = this.get(this.length - 1)
2
3    println("Kotlin".lastChar()) // Prints "n"
```

- **Scripting Capabilities**: Kotlin can be used as a scripting language. Kotlin scripts (.kts files) can be executed directly without the need for compilation, making it suitable for scripting and automation tasks.

31

In sum, Kotlin provides a blend of features that enhance developer productivity and application safety. Its conciseness reduces the time spent writing and maintaining code, its safety features help eliminate common programming errors, and its interoperability with Java protects and extends investments in Java technology. The support for coroutines, extension functions, and scripting further broadens Kotlin's applicability across different programming paradigms and use cases. These advantages make Kotlin a compelling choice for modern software development projects, from mobile and web development to server-side applications.

1.11   Common Use Cases for Kotlin

Kotlin, being a versatile and modern programming language, has found its usage across a broad spectrum of application development. Its concise syntax, safety features, and interoperability with Java allow developers to employ Kotlin in various domains efficiently. This section will discuss the most common use cases for Kotlin, including mobile development, server-side applications, desktop applications, web development, and data science.

Mobile Development

One of the primary applications of Kotlin is in mobile development, especially for Android. Since being officially supported by Google, Kotlin has become a go-to language for Android developers due to its conciseness and safety features over Java. The language's null safety and extension functions make Android APIs easier and safer to use, reducing the amount of boilerplate code and potential bugs.

```
1  fun showToast(context: Context, message: String) {
2      Toast.makeText(context, message, Toast.LENGTH_SHORT).show()
3  }
```

The above example demonstrates an extension function in Kotlin that simplifies showing a toast in Android applications.

Server-Side Applications

Kotlin is also widely used in the development of server-side applications. Its compatibility with existing Java libraries and frameworks, such as Spring Boot, Ktor, and Vert.x, makes it an increasingly popular choice for back-end development. Kotlin's coroutines feature offers a powerful tool for handling asynchronous operations, making server-side code more readable and maintainable.

```
1  fun main() = runBlocking<Unit> {
2      val data = async { fetchData() } // Fetch data asynchronously
3      println("Data fetched: ${data.await()}")
4  }
```

The snippet demonstrates the use of coroutines for asynchronous operations in Kotlin.

Desktop Applications

Kotlin can be used for developing cross-platform desktop applications. With the help of frameworks like TornadoFX, which is a lightweight JavaFX framework for Kotlin, creating rich and responsive desktop applications is straightforward. Kotlin's simplicity and the ability to interoperate with JavaFX make it a competent choice for desktop development.

Web Development

For web development, Kotlin offers Ktor and Kotlin/JS. Ktor is an asynchronous framework for creating microservices and web applications, focusing on simplicity and flexibility. Kotlin/JS, on the other hand, compiles Kotlin code to JavaScript, allowing developers to use Kotlin for front-end web development. This interoperability ensures that Kotlin can be employed both on the server and client-side, providing a full-stack development experience.

```
1  fun Application.module() {
2      routing {
3          get("/") {
4              call.respondText("Hello, world!", ContentType.Text.Html)
```

```
5           }
6       }
7   }
```

The example above illustrates the simplicity of setting up a basic web server with Ktor.

Data Science

While not as prevalent as Python, Kotlin is making strides in the data science domain. With libraries such as Krangl, which is a Kotlin library for data wrangling, and Kotlin for Apache Spark, which provides bindings for Kotlin to use Apache Spark, Kotlin is becoming an attractive option for data scientists who prefer static typing and the JVM ecosystem.

Kotlin's wide range of applications from mobile and server-side development to desktop and web applications, along with its growing use in data science, showcases the language's versatility. Its modern features and seamless interoperability with Java have positioned Kotlin as a powerful tool in a developer's arsenal for building efficient, safe, and concise applications across various domains.

Chapter 2

Setting up the Kotlin Development Environment

Establishing a robust development environment is the first step in beginning any Kotlin project. This encompasses installing the necessary tools, such as the Java Development Kit (JDK) and an Integrated Development Environment (IDE) that supports Kotlin, like IntelliJ IDEA or Android Studio. This chapter walks through the process of setting up these tools on various operating systems, configuring Kotlin in your chosen IDE, and ensuring that your environment is ready for both desktop and Android development. Additionally, it covers the management of dependencies and the use of build tools like Gradle, laying a solid foundation for efficient Kotlin development workflows.

2.1   Overview of Development Environment Requirements

Establishing a sound development environment is pivotal for the success of any project developed in Kotlin. This foundation entails the installation and configuration of several critical components, namely the Java Development Kit (JDK), an Integrated Development Environment (IDE) supportive of Kotlin coding, and essential tools like Gradle for managing dependencies and automating builds. This section delineates the essential requirements needed to create a robust Kotlin development setup conducive to both desktop and Android application development.

First and foremost, it is indispensable to have the Java Development Kit (JDK) installed on your machine. Kotlin runs on the Java Virtual Machine (JVM), making JDK a non-negotiable component for Kotlin development. The JDK provides the necessary ecosystem including the JVM, Java libraries, and tools essential for Kotlin compilation and execution. It's important to ensure that the JDK is correctly installed and that the environment variable is appropriately set up to reference the JDK installation directory.

Regarding the choice of Integrated Development Environment (IDE), Kotlin is markedly versatile. However, JetBrains' IntelliJ IDEA and Android Studio, given their direct support for Kotlin, emerge as the leading choices. Each of these IDEs comes with built-in support for Kotlin language, facilitating syntax highlighting, code completion, debugging, and additional features that enhance productivity. Installation processes for each IDE will vary slightly depending on the operating system, but generally involve executing the installer and following the setup wizard instructions.

Another cornerstone of a Kotlin development environment is the configuration of Gradle. Gradle is a powerful build automation tool that simplifies dependency management and custom build logic, indispensable for larger projects and Android development. Setting up Gradle within an IDE automates many tasks, such as compiling code, packaging binaries, and managing dependencies transparently.

- JDK installation and environment variable configuration

- Installation of an IDE that supports Kotlin (IntelliJ IDEA or Android Studio)

- Gradle for build automation and dependency management

Ensuring your development environment is correctly set up from the get-go paves the way for a smoother development process. This setup includes verifying the operational status of the JDK, as well as the installation and configuration of your preferred IDE and Gradle. Correct setup of these components not only streamlines the development process but also mitigates potential complications in project compilation and execution phases.

In summary, a well-established development environment forms the backbone of efficient and effective Kotlin development. This environment encompasses the Java Development Kit (JDK), an IDE that supports Kotlin, and Gradle for build automation. Each element plays a significant role in facilitating smooth Kotlin application development, warranting thoughtful installation and configuration.

2.2 Installing the Java Development Kit (JDK)

The Java Development Kit (JDK) is a prerequisite for running and developing Kotlin applications, as Kotlin compiles to Java Bytecode. Installation of the JDK is the foundation upon which the Kotlin development environment is built. This section will guide you through the process of downloading and installing the JDK on different operating systems.

Determining Your Operating System Version

Before downloading the JDK, it is essential to know your operating system's version, as different versions of the JDK are available for different operating systems and architectures. Execute the following command in your terminal or command prompt to determine your operating system version:

- For Windows: `systeminfo | findstr /B /C:"OS Name" /C:"OS Version"`

- For macOS: `sw_vers`

- For Linux: `lsb_release -a`

Downloading the JDK

Visit the official Oracle website to download the latest version of the JDK. Ensure that you select the appropriate version consistent with your operating system and architecture. Oracle provides JDK downloads as .exe files for Windows, .dmg files for macOS, and .tar.gz files for Linux.

Installation Process

Windows

1. Execute the downloaded .exe file to initiate the installation.

2. Follow the on-screen instructions, agreeing to the license agreement.

3. Choose an installation path. The default path is usually recommended.

4. Complete the installation and restart your computer if prompted.

macOS

1. Open the downloaded .dmg file and double-click the JDK installer.

2. Follow the on-screen instructions, agreeing to the license agreement.

3. The installer will install the JDK in the default location. You can change this location if necessary.

4. After installation, you may need to update your system's PATH environment variable to include the JDK.

Linux

For Linux, the process involves extracting the .tar.gz file and updating the PATH variable as follows:

```
1  $ tar -xvf jdk-<version>_linux-x64_bin.tar.gz
2  $ sudo mv jdk-<version> /usr/lib/jvm/jdk-<version>
3  $ export PATH=/usr/lib/jvm/jdk-<version>/bin:$PATH
```

Replace <version> with the actual version number of the JDK. Consider adding the export command to your profile script (.bashrc, .bash_profile, .zshrc, etc.) to ensure that the setting persists across sessions.

Verifying the Installation

To verify that the JDK has been installed successfully, open a terminal or command prompt and execute the following command:

```
java -version
```

The output should display the installed JDK version, verifying that the JDK is correctly installed on your system.

Setting JAVA_HOME Environment Variable

Setting the JAVA_HOME environment variable is a critical step that allows various tools and scripts to locate the JDK installation directory. This variable should point to the directory where the JDK is installed.

- For Windows, use the Environment Variables section in the System Properties.

- For macOS and Linux, add export JAVA_HOME=/path/to/jdk to your profile script.

Replace /path/to/jdk with the actual path to the JDK installation directory.

Ensuring that the JDK is installed correctly is vital for running and developing Kotlin applications. Following the steps outlined in this section will set up a robust foundation for your Kotlin development environment.

2.3   Setting Up Kotlin on IntelliJ IDEA

IntelliJ IDEA, created by JetBrains, is one of the most popular Integrated Development Environments (IDEs) for Kotlin development. Its robust feature set and tight integration with the Kotlin language make it an excellent choice for developers. This section will detail the steps necessary to configure Kotlin on IntelliJ IDEA, ensuring a seamless setup process.

First and foremost, it is imperative to have IntelliJ IDEA installed on your machine. The IDE offers two versions: the Community version, which is free and open-source, and the Ultimate version, which is paid and includes additional features. For Kotlin development, the Community version suffices. If IntelliJ IDEA is not yet installed, visit the official JetBrains website to download and install the Community version.

After successfully installing IntelliJ IDEA, launch the IDE to begin setting up Kotlin. The initial setup wizard may prompt you for basic IDE configurations. You can proceed with the default settings or adjust them to your preference.

Creating a New Kotlin Project

Once IntelliJ IDEA is ready, proceed to create a new Kotlin project by following these steps:

1. From the welcome screen or the File menu, select New > Project. This opens the New Project wizard.

2. In the New Project wizard, ensure Kotlin is selected on the left pane. You will see options for Kotlin/JVM, Kotlin/JS, and other project types. For most desktop applications, select Kotlin/JVM.

3. Specify the project's SDK. If you have previously installed Java Development Kit (JDK), IntelliJ IDEA should automatically detect and select it. If not, you may need to download and specify the path to the JDK.

4. Provide a name for your project and choose the project's location on your filesystem.

5. Click Finish to create your project. IntelliJ IDEA will initialize the project with a basic structure.

Exploring the Kotlin Project Structure

After creating a new Kotlin project, IntelliJ IDEA will display the project structure in the Project tool window. The primary components include:

- src - This directory contains the Kotlin source files (.kt) for your project.

- out - This directory is used by IntelliJ IDEA to store the compiled output of your project.

- External Libraries - Here, IntelliJ IDEA lists the libraries and SDKs referenced by your project, including the Kotlin standard library.

Configuring Kotlin Dependencies

IntelliJ IDEA automatically handles Kotlin dependencies for projects created using the New Project wizard. It includes the Kotlin standard library by default. However, to add additional libraries or manage project dependencies, you can use the Project Structure dialog:

1. Access the Project Structure dialog by navigating to File > Project Structure.

2. In the Libraries section, you can add or remove libraries to your project.

3. For Kotlin projects, you might particularly be interested in adding libraries such as Kotlinx Coroutines for asynchronous programming support.

Building and Running a Kotlin Application

With your Kotlin project set up in IntelliJ IDEA, you can now write a simple application to verify the setup:

```
1  fun main() {
2      println("Hello, Kotlin in IntelliJ IDEA!")
3  }
```

To run the application, right-click on the file containing the main function and select Run 'FileNameKt'. IntelliJ IDEA compiles the application and executes it, displaying the output in the Run tool window:

```
Hello, Kotlin in IntelliJ IDEA!
```

This verifies that your Kotlin environment is correctly set up in Intel-liJ IDEA, and you are ready to begin developing Kotlin applications.

2.4 Setting Up Kotlin on Android Studio

Setting up Kotlin on Android Studio is a straightforward process, thanks to the built-in support Kotlin has received from Android Studio since version 3.0. This integrated development environment (IDE) is tailored for Android development and provides all the necessary tools for building Android apps with Kotlin. This section covers the steps to configure Kotlin in Android Studio for both new and existing Android projects.

Prerequisites

Before proceeding with the setup, ensure that you have the latest version of Android Studio installed on your computer. If you are working with an older version, you may need to update it to access full Kotlin support.

Creating a New Kotlin Project

To start a new project in Kotlin:

- Open Android Studio and select File > New > New Project.

- In the Create New Project window, choose a project template. For beginners, the Empty Activity template is a suitable choice as it provides a minimal setup.

- Click Next.

- In the Configure your project section, make sure to select Kotlin in the Language dropdown menu.

- Fill out other project details such as Name, Save location, and Minimum API level.

- Click Finish. Android Studio will then create a new Kotlin project.

Adding Kotlin to an Existing Java Project

To add Kotlin to an existing Java project:

- Open your Java project in Android Studio.

- Navigate to Tools > Kotlin > Configure Kotlin in Project.

- Select the appropriate Kotlin compiler and runtime version for your project. Android Studio typically suggests the latest stable version.

- Click OK. Android Studio will then apply the necessary changes, including adding the Kotlin plugin and configuring the build scripts for Kotlin support.

Configuring the build.gradle File

For both new and existing projects, it's critical to ensure that the build.gradle files are properly configured for Kotlin. This involves two primary adjustments:

- Add the Kotlin Gradle plugin to the project-level build.gradle (Project: YourProjectName) file under dependencies:

```
1  classpath "org.jetbrains.kotlin:kotlin-gradle-plugin:$kotlin_version"
```

- In the module-level build.gradle (Module: app) file, apply the Kotlin Android plugin at the top:

```
1  apply plugin: 'kotlin-android'
```

- Also, add the Kotlin standard library dependency to the same file:

```
1  implementation "org.jetbrains.kotlin:kotlin-stdlib-jdk7:$kotlin_version"
```

Ensure that $kotlin_version matches the version of Kotlin that you are using in your project. This variable is typically defined in the project-level build.gradle file.

Running Your First Kotlin Application

Once the setup is complete, you can run your Kotlin application as you would any other Android app:

- Connect an Android device via USB or use the Android Emulator.
- Select the device in the Android Studio toolbar.
- Click the Run button or press Shift + F10.

If everything is configured correctly, your Kotlin application will launch on the selected device or emulator.

Additional Tips

- To convert existing Java code to Kotlin, right-click on the Java file in the Project pane and select Convert Java File to Kotlin File.
- Familiarize yourself with Kotlin-specific language features and best practices to maximize the productivity benefits Kotlin offers for Android development.

By following these steps, you have successfully set up Kotlin in Android Studio, empowering you to develop Android applications using this modern, concise, and safe programming language.

2.5   Using Kotlin with Eclipse

Eclipse is a widely used Integrated Development Environment (IDE) for Java development, and with the help of the Kotlin plugin, it can also serve as an efficient environment for Kotlin development. This section will guide you through the steps required to install and configure the Kotlin plugin for Eclipse, and subsequently demonstrate how to create and run a simple Kotlin application within Eclipse.

Installing the Kotlin Plugin for Eclipse

To begin, ensure that you have Eclipse installed on your system. The Kotlin plugin supports Eclipse Neon (4.6) or later. If you do not have Eclipse installed, download it from the official Eclipse Foundation website and follow the installation instructions relevant to your operating system.

Once Eclipse is installed and launched, proceed with the installation of the Kotlin plugin by following these steps:

- Open Eclipse and navigate to `Help > Eclipse Marketplace...`

- In the `Eclipse Marketplace` dialog, enter "Kotlin" in the search box and press Enter.

- Find the entry named "Kotlin Plugin for Eclipse" and click the `Install` button associated with it.

- Follow the prompts through the installation process, accepting licenses and confirming selected features.

- Restart Eclipse when prompted to complete the installation.

Creating a New Kotlin Project

With the Kotlin plugin installed, you can now create Kotlin projects in Eclipse. To create a new Kotlin project, follow these steps:

- From the Eclipse menu, select `File > New > Other...`

- In the `Select a wizard` dialog, expand the Kotlin folder, select `Kotlin Project`, and click `Next`.

- Name your project and configure any other necessary settings then click `Finish`.

This process will create a new Kotlin project in Eclipse with a default structure.

Writing and Running a Kotlin Application

To verify the setup, let us create and run a simple Kotlin application that prints "Hello, Kotlin" to the console.

- Right-click on the `src` folder of your newly created Kotlin project and select `New > Kotlin File`.

- Name the file `HelloKotlin` and click `Finish`.

- In the `HelloKotlin.kt` file that opens, enter the following code:

```
1  fun main(args: Array<String>) {
2      println("Hello, Kotlin")
3  }
```

- Right-click on the file in the Project Explorer and select `Run As > Kotlin Application`.

The output in the console should be:

```
Hello, Kotlin
```

This confirms that your Eclipse environment is correctly set up for Kotlin development. The Kotlin plugin for Eclipse includes features like syntax highlighting, code completion, debugging capabilities, and support for running Kotlin applications, making it a powerful tool for Kotlin development.

Using Eclipse for Kotlin development offers an accessible entry point for developers familiar with Java and the Eclipse IDE. By following the steps described in this section, developers can quickly set up their Eclipse environment for Kotlin development, leveraging Eclipse's extensive functionalities to create, develop, and manage Kotlin applications efficiently.

2.6 Configuring Kotlin in Visual Studio Code

Visual Studio Code (VS Code) is a powerful open-source code editor developed by Microsoft. While it does not come with built-in support for Kotlin out of the box, it can be turned into an efficient environment for Kotlin development with the help of extensions and appropriate configuration.   This section will discuss the step-by-step process to configure Kotlin in VS Code, which includes installing the Java Development Kit (JDK), the Kotlin Language extension, and configuring the build and run commands.

Firstly, ensure that the Java Development Kit (JDK) is installed on your machine.   Kotlin runs on the Java Virtual Machine (JVM), making the JDK a prerequisite for Kotlin development.   The installation process for the JDK has been covered in a previous section of this guide. After ensuring JDK is correctly set up, proceed with the following steps:

- Open Visual Studio Code.

- Navigate to the Extensions view by clicking on the square icon on the side menu or pressing Ctrl+Shift+X.

- In the Extensions search bar, type 'Kotlin'.

- Find the 'Kotlin Language' extension by fwcd and click the Install button.   This extension adds language support for Kotlin in VS Code, including syntax highlighting, code completion, and debugging features.

After installing the Kotlin Language extension, the next step is to set up the environment for compiling and running Kotlin applications. For this, it's necessary to use a build tool like Gradle or Maven, or to configure the Kotlin compiler directly. This guide will focus on using the Kotlin compiler directly for simplicity.

- Download the latest version of the Kotlin compiler from the official Kotlin website.

- Extract the downloaded .zip file to a convenient location on your filesystem.

- Add the `bin` directory of the extracted folder to your system's PATH environment variable to make the Kotlin compiler globally accessible from the command line.

With the Kotlin compiler set up, the next step is to configure VS Code to build and run Kotlin applications. This can be achieved by creating custom tasks in VS Code.

Create a new file named `tasks.json` inside the `.vscode` directory in your project's root. If the `.vscode` directory does not exist, you will need to create it. Add the following configuration to the `tasks.json` file:

```
1   {
2       "version": "2.0.0",
3       "tasks": [
4           {
5               "label": "Compile Kotlin",
6               "type": "shell",
7               "command": "kotlinc",
8               "args": [
9                   "${file}",
10                  "-include-runtime",
11                  "-d",
12                  "${fileDirname}/${fileBasenameNoExtension}.jar"
13              ],
14              "group": {
15                  "kind": "build",
16                  "isDefault": true
17              }
18          },
19          {
20              "label": "Run Kotlin",
21              "dependsOn": ["Compile Kotlin"],
22              "type": "shell",
23              "command": "java",
24              "args": [
25                  "-jar",
26                  "${fileDirname}/${fileBasenameNoExtension}.jar"
27              ]
28          }
29      ]
30  }
```

This configuration defines two tasks: one for compiling Kotlin files into a JAR file including the runtime, and the other for running the compiled JAR file. The ${file}, ${fileDirname}, and ${fileBasenameNoExtension} placeholders are substituted with the current file's path, directory, and name without extension, respectively, when the task is executed.

To run these tasks, open the Command Palette (Ctrl+Shift+P) and type 'Tasks: Run Task', then select either 'Compile Kotlin' or 'Run Kotlin' depending on your need.

With these steps completed, Visual Studio Code is now configured for Kotlin development. This configuration allows for composing, compiling, and executing Kotlin applications directly within the editor, leveraging VS Code's rich set of features for code editing and navigation.

For debugging support, it is currently necessary to rely on external tools or extensions that might become available in the future, as Kotlin-specific debugging features in VS Code are still under development at the time of writing.

2.7 Building and Running Your First Kotlin Application

In this section, we focus on the practical steps to build and execute a basic Kotlin application. This process involves creating a simple "Hello, World!" program, which is a traditional approach to introduce a new programming language. The simplicity of the "Hello, World!" program makes it an ideal starting point for beginners to understand the fundamental syntax and structure of Kotlin, as well as the procedure for compiling and running Kotlin programs.

To start, ensure that the Kotlin compiler is installed on your system. The Kotlin compiler can be obtained either by installing the standalone compiler from the Kotlin website or by ensuring it is bundled with your IDE, such as IntelliJ IDEA or Android Studio.

```
1  fun main() {
2      println("Hello, World!")
```

```
3    }
```

The code snippet above defines a Kotlin program that contains a single function, `main`, which is the entry point of a Kotlin application. Within this function, the `println()` method is used to print the text "Hello, World!" to the console.

To compile and run this Kotlin application, the following steps should be taken:

1. Open a terminal (command prompt) window.

2. Navigate to the directory where the Kotlin file is saved. Assume the Kotlin source file is named `HelloWorld.kt`.

3. Compile the Kotlin file to bytecode using the Kotlin compiler with the command:

```
1    kotlinc HelloWorld.kt -include-runtime -d HelloWorld.jar
```

   This command compiles the `HelloWorld.kt` file and includes the Kotlin runtime libraries in the output `.jar` file, which is necessary for running the Kotlin application.

4. Run the compiled application using the Java runtime with the command:

```
1    java -jar HelloWorld.jar
```

Upon successful compilation and execution, the output should display on the terminal as follows:

```
Hello, World!
```

This output confirms that the Kotlin application has been correctly compiled and executed, printing the intended message to the console.

Understanding the project structure in Kotlin is crucial for managing larger applications. Typically, a Kotlin project contains the following directories:

- `src/`: This directory contains all the Kotlin source files (.kt or .kts files).

- `lib/`: This is where the external libraries or dependencies are stored. These are necessary for providing additional functionalities that are not available in the standard library.

- `bin/`: Compiled bytecode files (.jar or .class files) are placed in this directory after the project is built.

In summary, building and running a Kotlin application involves writing the code, compiling it to bytecode, and executing the compiled bytecode with the Java runtime. The initial "Hello, World!" program serves as a gentle introduction to Kotlin's syntax and the process of compiling and running Kotlin applications. As a developer becomes more familiar with Kotlin, they can explore more complex programming constructs and utilize the rich set of features offered by the language to build sophisticated applications.

2.8   Understanding Kotlin Project Structure

When beginning a new Kotlin project, it's imperative to have a clear understanding of the basic project structure. This will facilitate easier navigation, management, and scalability of your Kotlin applications. The structure of a Kotlin project might appear daunting at first, but it follows a logical pattern that, once understood, becomes second nature.

A typical Kotlin project consists of several key components:

- **Source folders**: These are directories where your Kotlin source files (.kt) and resources are located.

- **The `src` directory**: This is the primary directory in a Kotlin project, and it typically contains two subdirectories, main and test.

- **The main directory**: Contains the actual source code (.kt files) and resources. It is often segregated into main/kotlin for the Kotlin source files and main/resources for the resource files such as XML configurations.

- **The test directory**: Holds the testing code which includes unit tests that help ensure your code works as expected. It similarly divides into test/kotlin for Kotlin test files and test/resources for resources required during testing.

- **The gradle directory and gradlew scripts**: These are part of the project setup when using Gradle as your build tool. The gradle directory contains Gradle wrapper scripts allowing the execution of Gradle tasks without requiring a system-wide Gradle installation.

- **The build directory**: This is generated when the project is built. It contains compiled classes and other output artifacts.

- **The .gradle and .idea directories**: These hidden directories contain configurations for Gradle and IntelliJ IDEA, respectively. They should not be manually edited in most cases.

- **Configuration files**: These include build.gradle or build.gradle.kts for Gradle, specifying project dependencies and build configurations, and settings.gradle or settings.gradle.kts for multi-project build configurations.

```
1  // Example of a simple Kotlin source file (Main.kt) residing in the
       src/main/kotlin` directory
2  fun main(args: Array<String>) {
3      println("Hello, Kotlin!")
4  }
```

```
Hello, Kotlin!
```

Understanding this structure is particularly useful for debugging issues related to resource loading or configuration. For instance, knowing that resource files should be placed under src/main/resources or `src/test/resources` can help solve problems where the application fails to locate these files at runtime.

Moreover, understanding the separation of source and test directories aids in maintaining clean code separation and organization, reinforcing best practices in software development. This structure not only ensures efficient compilation but also simplifies path configuration for different environments, ultimately leading to a more manageable and scalable project.

The organization of a Kotlin project into distinct directories and files serves several purposes. It streamlines development workflows, enhances code maintainability, facilitates team collaboration, and supports agile development practices by separating concerns and enabling modular growth. As you embark on Kotlin development, familiarize yourself with this structure to leverage these benefits fully.

2.9 Managing Dependencies in Kotlin Projects

In Kotlin projects, effectively managing dependencies is crucial for ensuring that your application is built upon reliable and up-to-date libraries while also maintaining compatibility between different components. Dependency management can become complex as your project grows, involving a myriad of libraries and frameworks. Kotlin, being interoperable with Java, allows leveraging a wide range of tools and libraries available for Java, in addition to Kotlin-specific resources.

The primary tool used for dependency management in Kotlin projects is Gradle. Gradle is a powerful build automation system that supports multi-language development, including Java and Kotlin. It facilitates declaring, resolving, and using dependencies in an efficient manner. To manage dependencies with Gradle, one must understand the structure of the `build.gradle` file and how to specify dependencies within it.

```
1  dependencies {
2      implementation "org.jetbrains.kotlin:kotlin-stdlib-jdk8:
           $kotlin_version"
3      testImplementation "junit:junit:4.13"
4  }
```

In the example above, two dependencies are added to the dependencies block of the build.gradle file. The 'implementation' keyword is used to add a library that is required for compiling and running your application. In this case, the Kotlin Standard Library compatible with Java 8 is added. The 'testImplementation' keyword specifies a dependency that is only used for compiling and running tests, such as JUnit.

To include a new library in your Kotlin project, follow these steps:

- Locate the library's Gradle dependency notation. This is usually provided in the library's documentation or in repositories like Maven Central or JCenter.

- Open the build.gradle file of your module.

- Add the dependency notation to the dependencies block, using either 'implementation' or 'testImplementation', depending on the use case.

- Sync your project with Gradle files to ensure that the new dependency is downloaded and available for use in your project.

Another important aspect of managing dependencies is to keep them up-to-date. Dependency versions are rapidly evolving, and using outdated libraries can expose your project to security vulnerabilities and compatibility issues. Gradle provides a convenient way to check for updates:

```
1  ./gradlew dependencyUpdates
```

This command, executed in the terminal within your project directory, uses the Gradle plugin 'com.github.ben-manes.versions' to report the availability of newer versions for your project dependencies.

It is advisable to periodically run this command and update your dependencies accordingly.

Moreover, managing transitive dependencies is another critical consideration. Transitive dependencies are the dependencies of the libraries that your project directly depends on. Gradle resolves these automatically by default, but conflicts can arise when different versions of the same library are included transitively. Gradle offers mechanisms such as dependency resolution strategies and exclusion rules to address these conflicts.

```
1  configurations.all {
2      resolutionStrategy.eachDependency { DependencyResolveDetails details
          ->
3          if (details.requested.group == 'com.fasterxml.jackson.core') {
4              details.useVersion '2.11.3'
5          }
6      }
7  }
```

The above script forces all sub-projects that depend on any 'com.fasterxml.jackson.core' module to use version '2.11.3', regardless of the requested version, preventing potential issues arising from version discrepancies.

Managing dependencies in Kotlin projects requires familiarity with Gradle and its capabilities. By effectively leveraging Gradle, developers can ensure that their projects are built upon a solid and up-to-date foundation of libraries, while also simplifying the build process and minimizing potential conflicts between dependencies.

2.10   Introduction to Gradle for Kotlin

Gradle is a powerful build automation tool that simplifies the process of building, testing, and deploying applications. Its flexibility and performance make it an ideal choice for projects written in Kotlin, among other languages. This section explores how Gradle facilitates Kotlin development by automating tedious tasks, managing dependencies, and integrating with various development environments.

To begin, install Gradle on your system. The installation process varies depending on the operating system. Ensure that Java is installed on your system, as Gradle requires it to run. After installation, verify the installation by running the following command in your terminal or command prompt:

```
1  gradle -v
```

This command displays the Gradle version, indicating a successful installation.

Gradle uses a build script to define the project and its tasks. For Kotlin projects, the build script is typically written in Kotlin DSL (Domain Specific Language), although Groovy DSL is also supported. The build script file is named 'build.gradle.kts' for Kotlin DSL.

The primary function of the Gradle build script in a Kotlin project is to define the project's configuration, including the following aspects:

- Project dependencies

- Compilation options

- Target platforms (JVM, Android, JavaScript)

- Testing frameworks

- Packaging and deployment settings

Defining dependencies is a crucial aspect of managing a Kotlin project with Gradle. Dependencies are external libraries your project requires to function. Gradle simplifies dependency management by retrieving these libraries from online repositories, such as Maven Central or JCenter, and including them in your project. To add a dependency, you specify it in the dependencies block of your 'build.gradle.kts' file:

```
1  dependencies {
2      implementation("org.jetbrains.kotlin:kotlin-stdlib-jdk8:
           $kotlin_version")
```

```
3   }
```

This line adds the Kotlin standard library compatible with Java 8 to the project. The $kotlin_version variable should be defined in the 'gradle.properties' file or directly in the build script.

Building and running a Kotlin application with Gradle is straightforward. Use the following command to compile your project:

```
1   gradle build
```

To run your application, if it has a main method, use:

```
1   gradle run
```

Gradle will compile the Kotlin code, run any defined tests, and execute the application if the build is successful.

Gradle also supports multi-project builds, where a single build script can manage multiple subprojects. This feature is particularly useful for large Kotlin applications that consist of multiple modules.

Gradle offers robust and flexible build automation for Kotlin projects. By automating the build process, managing dependencies, and integrating with development environments, Gradle enhances productivity and streamlines the development workflow. With the information provided in this section, setting up a Kotlin project with Gradle should be an efficient and straightforward process.

2.11   Using the Kotlin Command Line Compiler

While Integrated Development Environments (IDEs) offer comprehensive facilities for Kotlin development, understanding and utilizing the Kotlin Command Line Compiler can significantly enhance a developer's versatility and efficiency.   This section explores how to use the Kotlin compiler directly from the command line, enabling the compilation of Kotlin code into Java bytecode without the need for an IDE.

To begin, ensure that the Kotlin compiler is installed and accessible on your system. The Kotlin compiler can be obtained through the Kotlin website or through package managers on certain operating systems.

Commands to install the Kotlin compiler vary based on the operating system:

- On Ubuntu-based Linux distributions, you can use sudo apt-get install kotlin.
- On macOS, using Homebrew, the command is brew install kotlin.
- For Windows, downloading and running the installer from the Kotlin website is recommended.

After installation, verify the compiler's availability by running kotlinc -version in the terminal. Successful installation will show the version of the Kotlin compiler.

Compiling a Single Kotlin File

To compile a single Kotlin file, use the kotlinc command followed by the file name. For example, to compile a file named Main.kt, the command would be:

```
1  kotlinc Main.kt -include-runtime -d Main.jar
```

This command compiles Main.kt into a JAR file named Main.jar, including the Kotlin runtime in the JAR to ensure it can run on any Java virtual machine. The -d option specifies the output directory or file name.

Executing the Compiled Kotlin Program

Once compiled, the Kotlin program can be executed using the Java Runtime Environment (JRE). To run Main.jar, the command is:

```
1   java -jar Main.jar
```

The output of the Kotlin program will be displayed in the terminal.

Compiling Multiple Kotlin Files

For projects with multiple Kotlin files, specify all files in the `kotlinc` command. Assume a project with two Kotlin files: `Main.kt` and `Utility.kt`. The command to compile these files is:

```
1   kotlinc Main.kt Utility.kt -include-runtime -d Project.jar
```

Using Kotlin with Scripts

Kotlin also supports scripting functionality. Kotlin scripts have a `.kts` extension and can be executed directly using the `kotlinc` command without explicitly compiling them first. For example, to run a script named `script.kts`, the command is:

```
1   kotlinc -script script.kts
```

This command parses and directly executes the Kotlin script.

Troubleshooting Compilation Errors

Common issues encountered during compilation include syntax errors, missing dependencies, and incompatible Kotlin versions. The Kotlin compiler provides detailed error messages to assist in troubleshooting these problems. For each error, the compiler will output the file name, line number, and a description of the issue, facilitating rapid debugging.

Using the Kotlin Command Line Compiler offers a lightweight, flexible approach to Kotlin development, suitable for scenarios ranging from simple script execution to complex project compilation. Mastery of command line compilation techniques empowers developers to automate Kotlin compilation processes, integrate Kotlin into varied development pipelines, and understand the foundational aspects of Kotlin execution without reliance on an IDE.

2.12 Troubleshooting Common Setup Issues

Dealing with setup issues can be a frustrating part of starting with any new programming language, including Kotlin. This section will outline common problems encountered during the setup process of the Kotlin development environment and provide solutions to efficiently resolve them.

JDK Is Not Recognized

One of the first hurdles you might encounter is that your Integrated Development Environment (IDE) does not recognize the Java Development Kit (JDK). This issue typically arises from either not having the JDK installed or the development environment not being correctly pointed toward the JDK's installation directory.

- First, verify if JDK is installed on your system by opening a terminal and executing:

```
1  java -version
```

If this command does not return the version of Java installed, you need to install the JDK.

- If JDK is installed, you need to configure your IDE to recognize the JDK path. This can usually be done in the Project Structure or System Settings of the IDE, under the SDKs or JDKs section.

Kotlin Plugin Not Detected or Outdated

Integrating Kotlin into IDEs such as IntelliJ IDEA or Android Studio requires the Kotlin plugin. An undetected or outdated plugin can prevent you from starting or building Kotlin projects.

- Verify that the Kotlin plugin is installed by accessing the plugin settings in your IDE. This is typically found under Settings > Plugins.

- If the plugin is missing, search for Kotlin in the plugin marketplace and install it.

- If the plugin is installed but the issue persists, check if there is an update available for the plugin and update accordingly.

Gradle Sync Failure

Gradle is an essential tool for managing dependencies and automating builds in Kotlin projects. However, problems such as failed syncs can occur, especially in Android development.

- Review the Gradle output pane for specific error messages. Issues often stem from incompatible versions between the Gradle wrapper and the Kotlin plugin.

- Ensure that your build.gradle file specifies a compatible Kotlin version.

```
1  dependencies {
2      classpath "org.jetbrains.kotlin:kotlin-gradle-plugin:
           $kotlin_version"
3  }
```

- In case of version incompatibility, update the Kotlin version in your project's build.gradle file to match the version supported by the plugin.

Problems with Kotlin Command Line Compiler

Sometimes, compiling Kotlin programs from the command line might fail due to various issues, such as incorrect setup or PATH environment variable problems.

- Ensure that the Kotlin compiler `kotlinc` is correctly installed and accessible from your command line. You can test this by running:

```
1  kotlinc -version
```

- If the command is unrecognized, add the Kotlin compiler's bin directory to your system's PATH variable. The exact steps vary by operating system, but generally involve editing system environment settings.

Final Recommendations

Addressing setup issues often requires a methodical approach to identify the root cause. Always ensure that your tools and plugins are up to date, and consult the official Kotlin documentation and community forums for specific problems and solutions. Understanding the common setup issues and their resolutions will streamline your development workflow, allowing you to focus more on writing Kotlin code than troubleshooting environment setup problems.

Chapter 3

Kotlin Syntax and Basic Programming Concepts

Grasping the syntax and fundamental programming concepts of Kotlin is crucial for effective development in this language. This chapter introduces the basic building blocks of Kotlin, including variables, data types, control flow statements, and functions. It emphasizes the language's type system, null safety features, and the concise ways to handle data and operations, which are pivotal in writing clean, robust, and efficient code. Through this exploration, readers will gain an understanding of how to structure Kotlin programs and utilize its syntax to express programming logic clearly and succinctly, setting a solid base for more advanced topics.

3.1 Understanding Basic Syntax

In this section, we will discuss the core syntax components of the Kotlin programming language. Understanding the syntax is fundamental, as it is the foundation upon which all Kotlin programs are built.

Firstly, every Kotlin file, often referred to as a source file, is identified by its `.kt` extension. Kotlin programs can consist of one or more source files, and one of these files must contain a `main` function, which serves as the entry point of the program.

```
fun main() {
    println("Hello, world!")
}
```

In the example above, `main` is a function that takes no parameters and returns no value. It prints the string "Hello, world!" to the standard output.

Kotlin's syntax emphasizes conciseness and safety. One of the first things you'll notice is the type inference capability. While you can explicitly specify types, Kotlin can often infer them, making your code cleaner and more concise.

```
val greeting = "Hello, world!"
println(greeting)
```

In the snippet above, `greeting` is implicitly recognized as a `String` without explicitly declaring its type.

Variables in Kotlin are introduced using either the `val` or `var` keyword. `val` declares a read-only (immutable) variable, meaning once it has been assigned a value, it cannot be reassigned. `var` declares a mutable variable, which can be reassigned.

```
val immutableVariable = "I cannot be changed"
var mutableVariable = "I can be changed"
mutableVariable = "See, I changed!"
```

Kotlin enforces strict typing, yet it offers a null-safe type system. Variables cannot hold a null value unless explicitly declared.

```
var nullableString: String? = null
var nonNullableString: String = "I cannot be null"
```

Control flow statements in Kotlin include `if`, `when`, `for`, and `while`. The `if` expression may return a value, allowing it to be used in assignments.

```
1  val max = if (a > b) a else b
```

Functions in Kotlin are defined using the fun keyword and can have parameters and return types. Parameters are specified after the function name, inside parentheses. The return type, if present, is specified after a colon.

```
1  fun sum(a: Int, b: Int): Int {
2      return a + b
3  }
```

Lastly, Kotlin supports single-line comments with // and multi-line comments between /* and */.

```
1  // This is a single-line comment.
2  /* This is a
3     multi-line comment. */
```

Understanding these basic syntax elements is crucial for developing proficiency in Kotlin. In subsequent sections, we will delve deeper into each of these concepts and explore how they are used in practical programming scenarios.

3.2   Declaring Variables and Types

In this section, we will discuss the essentials of declaring variables and understanding types in Kotlin. Kotlin's type inference system allows for concise code, yet it is fundamental to grasp how to explicitly define types when necessary.

Kotlin gives developers the flexibility to declare variables using either the val keyword for read-only (immutable) variables or the var keyword for mutable variables. The choice between val and var is pivotal in Kotlin's approach to more predictable and less error-prone code, as it encourages the use of immutable variables whenever possible.

To declare a variable in Kotlin, you may either explicitly specify its type or allow the compiler to infer it. Here's how you can declare a variable with type inference:

```
1  val playerName = "Alex"
2  var score = 10
```

Notice that we haven't specified the types of playerName and score. Kotlin infers playerName to be of type String and score of type Int.

Now, let's see how to declare variables with explicit types:

```
1  val playerName: String = "Alex"
2  var score: Int = 10
```

Explicit type declarations are particularly useful in scenarios where you want your code to be self-documenting, or when the variable is declared without initialization.

Kotlin's strong type system also embraces nullability as part of the type. Variables in Kotlin are non-null by default. To declare a variable that can hold a null value, you must explicitly mark the type as nullable by adding a question mark (?) after the type name.

```
1  var playerName: String? = null
```

Updating or accessing a nullable variable necessitates careful handling to avoid the dreaded NullPointerException. Kotlin provides a range of options for dealing with null values safely, including safe calls (?.) and the Elvis operator (?:).

Let's delve into Kotlin's type hierarchy. At the top of the hierarchy is Any, which is the root of all non-nullable types. The nullable counterpart is Any?. Kotlin also provides a special type, Unit, for functions that do not return a meaningful value (analogous to void in Java).

- Primitives: Unlike Java, Kotlin does not have separate namespaces for primitive types and their boxed counterparts. Types like Int, Double, and Boolean are represented as objects. However, the Kotlin compiler optimizes the usage of these types to use primitive types when possible.

- Strings: Strings in Kotlin are immutable sequences of characters. String templates or string interpolation allows the embedding of expressions within string literals.

- Arrays: Kotlin treats arrays as a class, `Array`, which contains get and set functions, along with other useful member functions.

One of the benefits of the strong type system in Kotlin is the reduced likelihood of type errors in your code. Furthermore, the explicit handling of nullability aids in preventing runtime errors due to null reference exceptions.

In summary, understanding how to declare variables and types in Kotlin is crucial for writing effective Kotlin code. By choosing between `val` and `var` wisely, making use of type inference, and handling nullability properly, you can take advantage of Kotlin's features to write cleaner, more reliable code.

3.3 Working with Strings and Characters

In this section, we will discuss the manipulation and management of strings and characters in Kotlin, which are fundamental in almost every programming task, from displaying messages to processing text data.

Kotlin treats strings as sequences of characters. A string can be declared in the same way as primitives, using the `String` type. Characters, on the other hand, are declared using the `Char` type. Let's start by looking at how to declare strings and characters.

```
1  val exampleString: String = "Hello, Kotlin!"
2  val exampleChar: Char = 'K'
```

Strings in Kotlin are immutable. This means that once a string is created, it cannot be changed. Operations on strings, such as concatenation or trimming, result in a new string.

String Operations

Several operations can be performed on strings, including accessing characters, concatenation, interpolation, and iteration over characters.

Accessing Characters: You can access characters in a string by their index using square bracket syntax.

```
1   val charAtIndex = exampleString[7] // Accessing the 8th character,
        which is 'K'
```

Concatenation: Strings can be concatenated using the + operator.

```
1   val greeting = "Hello, " + "Kotlin!"
```

String Interpolation: Kotlin supports string interpolation, allowing the insertion of variable values or expressions directly into a string.

```
1   val name = "Kotlin"
2   val greeting = "Hello, $name!"
```

Iteration Over Characters: You can iterate over all characters in a string using a for loop.

```
1   for (char in exampleString) {
2       println(char)
3   }
```

Escape Sequences

Strings can contain special characters, known as escape sequences. These are used to represent characters that cannot be typed directly into a string, such as newline or tab.

```
1   val stringWithEscapeSequences = "Hello,\nKotlin!\tThis is an example."
```

Here,
n represents a newline, and
t represents a tab.

Raw Strings

Kotlin also supports raw strings, which are useful for strings that span multiple lines or contain special characters. Raw strings are enclosed in triple quotes (""" """) and do not process escape sequences.

```
1  val rawString = """
2     This is a raw string.
3     It spans multiple lines.
4     No need for \n escape sequences.
5  """
```

String Methods

Kotlin provides a rich set of methods for working with strings, including functions for trimming, padding, splitting, and matching. Here is an example of using some common string methods.

```
1  val originalString = " Kotlin Programming "
2
3  // Trim leading and trailing spaces
4  val trimmedString = originalString.trim()
5
6  // Check if a string contains a substring
7  val containsSubstring = originalString.contains("Prog")
8
9  // Replace a substring with another string
10 val replacedString = originalString.replace("Programming", "
       Development")
```

Utilizing these string operations effectively allows for the robust manipulation and analysis of textual data in Kotlin applications.

3.4 Working with Numbers and Arithmetic Operations

In this section, we will discuss how to work with numbers and perform arithmetic operations in Kotlin. Kotlin provides a comprehensive set of data types to represent numbers and allows for a wide range of arithmetic operations to be performed on them.

Number Data Types in Kotlin

Kotlin supports the following number data types:

- Byte: An 8-bit signed integer.

- Short: A 16-bit signed integer.

- Int: A 32-bit signed integer.

- Long: A 64-bit signed integer.

- Float: A 32-bit floating-point number.

- Double: A 64-bit floating-point number.

Each of these data types is used to represent numbers with varying ranges and precisions. It's important to choose the appropriate type based on the requirements of the operation to maximize efficiency and avoid overflow or precision loss.

Arithmetic Operations

Kotlin supports the standard set of arithmetic operations: addition, subtraction, multiplication, division, and modulus. The following examples demonstrate these operations:

```
1   val a = 10
2   val b = 3
3
4   // Addition
5   val sum = a + b
6
7   // Subtraction
8   val difference = a - b
9
10  // Multiplication
```

```
11    val product = a * b
12
13    // Division
14    val quotient = a / b
15
16    // Modulus
17    val remainder = a % b
```

It is important to note that when performing division with integers, the result is truncated towards zero. To obtain a floating-point result, at least one of the operands must be a floating-point number.

Arithmetic Operations with Floating-Point Numbers

Working with floating-point numbers is similar to working with integers, but it is essential to be aware of precision issues that can arise. Here is an example of arithmetic operations with floating-point numbers:

```
1    val x = 10.5
2    val y = 3.5
3
4    // Floating-point division
5    val floatingQuotient = x / y
6
7    // Modulus
8    val floatingRemainder = x % y
```

```
floatingQuotient: 3.0
floatingRemainder: 0.5
```

Unlike integer division, division with floating-point numbers does not truncate the result, as both operands are capable of representing fractions.

Increment and Decrement Operators

Kotlin also provides increment (++) and decrement (--) operators, which increase or decrease a variable's value by one, respectively. These operators can be used in both prefix and postfix forms.

```
1  var counter = 0
2
3  // Prefix increment
4  ++counter
5
6  // Postfix decrement
7  counter--
```

In the prefix form, the variable is incremented or decremented before its value is used in the expression. In the postfix form, the original value of the variable is used in the expression, and then the variable is incremented or decremented.

To summarize, Kotlin's support for arithmetic operations allows for efficient and precise numeric calculations. Understanding how to use these operations with different data types is crucial for performing mathematical tasks in Kotlin.

3.5   Control Flow: if, when, for, while

Control flow statements in Kotlin, namely if, when, for, and while, are essential for directing the flow of execution in a program. These structures allow for conditional execution of code blocks and looping, which are fundamental in creating dynamic and responsive applications.

The if Statement

The if statement in Kotlin is straightforward and similar to its counterparts in many other programming languages. It evaluates a condition, which is an expression that returns a Boolean value (true or false). Depending on the result, it then executes a specific block of code.

```
1  val number = 5
2  if (number > 0) {
3      println("The number is positive")
4  } else {
```

```
5        println("The number is not positive")
6    }
```

`if` can also be used as an expression, returning a value. This is particularly useful for assigning variables based on conditional logic.

```
1    val result = if (number > 100) "large" else "small"
2    println("The number is $result")
```

The when Expression

Kotlin introduces a powerful control flow statement called `when`, which simplifies complex `if-else if` chains. It works by matching its argument against all branches sequentially until some branch condition is satisfied.

```
1    val score = 76
2    when (score) {
3        in 90..100 -> println("Excellent")
4        in 80..89 -> println("Good")
5        in 70..79 -> println("Average")
6        else -> println("Fail")
7    }
```

`when` can also be used as a replacement for an `if-else` chain when there are multiple conditions to check against a single value.

Looping with for and while

Kotlin provides two types of loops for iterating over ranges, collections, or anything that provides an iterator: `for` and `while`.

The for Loop

The `for` loop in Kotlin is used to iterate over ranges or collections. It is more flexible and concise compared to traditional `for` loops found in other languages.

```
1    for (i in 1..5) {
```

```
2        println(i)
3    }
```

It can also be used to iterate over collections and arrays.

```
1    val fruits = listOf("apple", "banana", "cherry")
2    for (fruit in fruits) {
3        println(fruit)
4    }
```

The while and do-while Loops

The while loop executes a block of code repeatedly as long as a given condition is true. The condition is evaluated before each iteration.

```
1    var x = 10
2    while (x > 0) {
3        println(x)
4        x--
5    }
```

The do-while loop is similar to the while loop, but it ensures that the block of code is executed at least once, as the condition is checked after the block execution.

```
1    do {
2        println(x)
3        x++
4    } while (x < 20)
```

These control flow constructs are foundational in Kotlin programming. They give developers the ability to make decisions, execute code based on conditions, and perform repetitive tasks efficiently. It is crucial to understand and utilize these constructs appropriately to develop logical and concise Kotlin applications.

3.6   Creating and Using Functions

Creating functions in Kotlin is an essential aspect of writing concise and maintainable code. Functions allow developers to encapsulate reusable code blocks that perform specific operations. This section elucidates the process of declaring and using functions in Kotlin, including understanding function syntax, parameters, return types, and default arguments, facilitating the crafting of modular and cleaner codebases.

In Kotlin, a function is declared using the `fun` keyword, followed by the function name, a pair of parentheses (which may contain parameters), and the return type of the function. The body of the function is enclosed in curly braces. Here is a basic example of a function declaration in Kotlin:

```
1  fun greet(): Unit {
2      println("Hello, World!")
3  }
```

The above function, named `greet`, does not take any parameters and does not return any value (denoted by `Unit`, which is similar to `void` in other programming languages). When called, it simply prints "Hello, World!" to the standard output.

Function Parameters and Return Types

To make functions more flexible and useful, we can define parameters that the function can accept and specify the type of value that the function will return. Consider a function that takes two `Int` parameters and returns their sum:

```
1  fun sum(a: Int, b: Int): Int {
2      return a + b
3  }
```

Calling the `sum` function with two integers will return their sum:

```
val result = sum(5, 3)
println(result)  // Output: 8
```

77

Default Arguments and Named Parameters

Kotlin provides features like default arguments and named parameters to enhance the flexibility of function calls. Default arguments allow you to specify default values for parameters, making them optional when calling the function. Here is an example that demonstrates this feature:

```
1  fun greet(name: String, greeting: String = "Hello") {
2      println("$greeting, $name!")
3  }
```

With the greet function, the greeting parameter is optional due to the default value "Hello". This enables the function to be called in two ways:

```
greet("John")                   // Output: Hello, John!
greet("John", "Good morning")   // Output: Good morning, John!
```

Named parameters allow the caller of a function to specify the values for parameters explicitly by name. This is particularly useful when a function has a large number of parameters or default values. For instance:

```
1  fun configureNetwork(host: String, port: Int = 80, ssl: Boolean =
       false) {
2      // Function body
3  }
```

This function can be invoked with named parameters as follows:

```
configureNetwork(host = "example.com", ssl = true)
```

By using named parameters, the code becomes more readable, and the order of the arguments can be altered without affecting the functionality.

Single-Expression Functions

Kotlin supports single-expression functions, allowing functions with a simple expression to be more concisely written. In this form, the curly braces of the function body are replaced by an equals sign followed by the expression. The return type is inferred by the compiler:

```
1  fun square(x: Int) = x * x
```

The square function takes an Int parameter and returns its square, with the return type Int inferred automatically.

To summarize, functions in Kotlin are defined using the fun keyword followed by the function name, parameters, and return type. Kotlin enhances function declaration and usage through features such as default arguments, named parameters, and single-expression functions, thus promoting code readability and maintainability.

3.7 Understanding Nullability and Safe Calls

Kotlin is a statically typed programming language that emphasizes safety, including null safety, to prevent the common 'NullPointerException' that often plagues Java applications. A key feature of Kotlin is its system for nullability and safe calls, which allows developers to write more reliable code with fewer crashes.

Nullable Types

In Kotlin, every variable and reference has a type which determines the kind of values it can hold. By default, variables in Kotlin cannot hold null. This feature substantially reduces the risk of null pointer errors. However, there are cases when a variable needs to hold a null value. For such cases, Kotlin provides nullable types.

To declare a variable as nullable, append a question mark to the type:

```
1  var name: String? = null
```

This code snippet declares a variable name of type String?, indicating that name can hold a string value or be null.

Safe Calls Operator (?.)

While nullable types are useful, they require careful handling. The safe call operator ?. allows you to access properties or call methods on a nullable object safely.   If the object is not null, the property/method is accessed/called; if it is null, the operation returns null without throwing a 'NullPointerException'.

Example usage:

```
1  val length = name?.length
```

In this snippet, name is a nullable string. The ?. operator is used to safely access its length property. If name is null, length will be set to null instead of throwing an exception.

The Elvis Operator (?:)

What if you want to provide a default value in case a nullable object is found to be null? This is what the Elvis operator ?: is for. It allows you to specify a fallback value to use in case the left-hand side expression is null.

For instance:

```
1  val length = name?.length ?: 0
```

Here, if name is null, rather than assigning null to length, it is assigned a default value of 0.

Not-null Assertion Operator (!!.)

In situations where you are absolutely sure that a nullable object is not null, you can use the not-null assertion operator !!. This operator converts any value to a non-null type and throws an exception if the value is null.

Example:

```
1   val length = name!!.length
```

This will return the length of `name` if `name` is not null; otherwise, it throws a 'NullPointerException'.

Safe Casts: as?

Finally, Kotlin provides the safe cast operator `as?`, which safely casts a variable to the specified type. If the variable cannot be cast, the operation returns null instead of throwing a `ClassCastException`.

Example:

```
1   val x: Any = "Kotlin"
2   val y: String? = x as? String
```

In this case, x is safely cast to a String and assigned to y. If the cast was not possible, y would be null.

This section details the mechanisms Kotlin provides for handling nullability safely, including the use of nullable types, the safe call operator (?,), the Elvis operator (?:), the not-null assertion operator (!!.), and safe casts with the operator (as?). These features enable developers to write more reliable code with explicit null handling, reducing the occurrences of 'NullPointerExceptions'.

3.8 Using Lambdas and Higher-Order Functions

Lambdas and higher-order functions are pivotal in facilitating a functional programming approach within Kotlin. This section will delve into the utilization of these constructs, showcasing their efficacy in writing concise code while maintaining readability and flexibility.

Lambdas, or lambda expressions, are essentially anonymous functions that can be treated as values: passed to, returned from functions, or stored in variables. The general syntax for a lambda expression in Kotlin is as follows:

```
1  { parameters -> body }
```

For instance, a basic lambda that takes two integers and returns their sum can be defined as:

```
1  val sum: (Int, Int) -> Int = { a, b -> a + b }
```

In the above example, sum is a variable of a function type (Int, Int) -> Int, which implies it takes two integers as parameters and returns an integer. The lambda expression is provided on the right side of the assignment.

Moving to higher-order functions, these are functions that take other functions as parameters or return them. The power of higher-order functions is evident in Kotlin's standard library, which is replete with such functions that operate on collections, among other things. An example is the map function, which applies a given transformation to each element in a collection.

To illustrate, consider the following list of numbers and a task to square each number:

```
1  val numbers = listOf(1, 2, 3, 4, 5)
2  val squaredNumbers = numbers.map { it * it }
```

Here, map is a higher-order function that takes a lambda expressing the transformation to apply. The keyword it represents each element in the list during the iteration.

Lambdas in Kotlin can also access variables from the outer scope, known as closure. This feature allows lambdas to work on data outside their scope, providing a flexible way to handle data manipulation without requiring additional parameters. However, it's essential to manage outer scope variables cautiously to avoid unintended modifications.

A compelling aspect of lambdas and higher-order functions in Kotlin is their support for inline functions. When a higher-order function is marked as inline, the compiler will not create a function object for the lambda. Instead, it will replace the higher-order function call with the lambda body. This optimization technique reduces memory overhead and runtime costs associated with function calls and object creation.

Kotlin's type inference capability often allows for the omission of explicit types, making the code cleaner and less verbose. Consequently, the readability of lambda expressions and higher-order functions improves, as seen in the following example employing the `filter` and `map` functions:

```
1   val positiveSquaredNumbers = numbers.filter { it > 0 }.map { it * it }
```

In this case, `filter` removes any numbers less than or equal to zero, and `map` squares the remaining numbers. Both operations are connected in a concise statement demonstrating the power of combining lambdas with higher-order functions for data processing.

In summary, lambdas and higher-order functions significantly enhance Kotlin's programming model. They offer an expressive mechanism to encapsulate operations as values, facilitate operations on collections, and enable a functional style of programming that is both succinct and expressive. Understanding and leveraging these constructs is essential for Kotlin developers aiming to write efficient, clean, and maintainable code.

3.9 Introduction to Collections: List, Set, and Map

Collections in Kotlin are a fundamental part of storing groups of related objects. They are especially useful when you need to group objects in a single entity, manage and process them collectively. Kotlin provides a rich set of collection types, each designed for specific purposes. In this section, we will focus on three primary collection types: List, Set, and Map.

List

A List is an ordered collection that can store multiple elements, including duplicates. Elements in a List have a specific sequence, and they can be accessed by their index, which starts from zero.

Here is how you can create and manipulate a List in Kotlin:

```
val names: List<String> = listOf("Anna", "Brian", "Craig", "Anna")
println(names[2]) // Access element by index, prints "Craig"
```

The output of the code will be:

```
Craig
```

Lists in Kotlin are immutable by default, meaning once a list is created, its elements cannot be changed. However, Kotlin also provides a mutable version, MutableList, which allows adding, removing, or updating its elements.

Set

A Set is a collection that holds unique elements. It is particularly useful when you need to ensure that there are no duplicate elements in the collection. Like Lists, Sets also have their mutable version.

An example of creating and using a Set:

```
val uniqueNames: Set<String> = setOf("Anna", "Brian", "Craig", "Anna")
println(uniqueNames.size) // Prints the size of the Set, duplicates
    are ignored
```

The output for the above code snippet will be:

```
3
```

This demonstrates the uniqueness property of the Set collection - even though "Anna" is added twice, the Set considers it only once.

84

Map

A Map is a collection of key-value pairs where each key maps to a specific value. Keys in a Map are unique, and each key can map to exactly one value. Maps are useful when you need to retrieve values based on their keys.

Creating and using a Map in Kotlin:

```
1  val countryCodes: Map<String, String> = mapOf("USA" to "US", "India"
       to "IN", "China" to "CN")
2  println(countryCodes["USA"]) // Access value by key
```

The output here is:

```
US
```

Like Lists and Sets, Maps also come in mutable versions, allowing the addition, removal, and update of pairs.

Choosing the Right Collection

Choosing the correct type of collection depends on the specific requirements of the program. Here are some guidelines:

- Use List when you need ordered collection with possibly duplicate elements.

- Use Set when you must ensure uniqueness of elements.

- Use Map when you need to associate keys to values.

Understanding these collections and their proper usage is crucial for effective Kotlin programming. Each collection type serves its unique purpose, and selecting the appropriate one can lead to more efficient, readable, and maintainable code.

3.10   Basic File I/O in Kotlin

File Input/Output (I/O) operations are foundational in many programming tasks, allowing programs to persist data between sessions or to read configuration and data files. Kotlin provides a straightforward and efficient way to perform file operations, leveraging the capabilities of the Java I/O classes through the Kotlin standard library. This section explores the basic file I/O operations in Kotlin, including reading from and writing to files.

Reading Files

In Kotlin, reading a file can be performed succinctly with the `readText()` method for small files, or with `bufferedReader()` for larger files, to manage memory more efficiently.

```kotlin
import java.io.File

fun readFileAsString(filePath: String): String {
    return File(filePath).readText(Charsets.UTF_8)
}

fun readLargeFile(filePath: String) {
    File(filePath).bufferedReader().use { reader ->
        var line: String?
        while (reader.readLine().also { line = it } != null) {
            println(line)
        }
    }
}
```

The `readText()` method reads the entire file content into a String. It's convenient but not suitable for large files due to memory constraints. The `bufferedReader()` method, used with a while loop, reads the file line by line, making it more memory-efficient for larger files.

Writing Files

Writing to files in Kotlin can also be accomplished with methods like `writeText()` for writing a complete string to a file, or `bufferedWriter()` for writing larger data by chunks or line by line.

```
1  import java.io.File
2
3  fun writeStringToFile(filePath: String, content: String){
4      File(filePath).writeText(content)
5  }
6
7  fun writeLargeDataToFile(filePath: String, data: List<String>) {
8      File(filePath).bufferedWriter().use { out ->
9          data.forEach { line ->
10             out.write(line)
11             out.newLine()
12         }
13     }
14 }
```

The `writeText()` method simplifies the process of writing a complete string to a file, replacing any existing content. The `bufferedWriter()` method provides a more granular control for writing data, useful for larger files or when appending to a file is needed.

It is essential to handle file operations with appropriate error handling mechanisms to manage exceptions that may arise. For instance, attempting to read from a non-existent file or facing access permission issues. Kotlin's try-catch blocks can be effectively used to handle these exceptions gracefully.

```
1  try {
2      val content = readFileAsString("path/to/file.txt")
3      println(content)
4  } catch (e: Exception) {
5      println("An error occurred: ${e.message}")
6  }
```

In summary, Kotlin simplifies file I/O operations through its standard library, providing a clean and concise way to perform these common tasks. By understanding how to read and write files in Kotlin, developers can handle a wide range of programming scenarios, from simple configurations to complex data processing tasks.

3.11 Exception Handling in Kotlin

Exception handling in Kotlin operates on the principle of catching exceptions that may arise during the execution of a program, thereby preventing the program from abruptly terminating. Kotlin's approach is similar to Java, but with some syntactic and functional improvements that make exception handling more concise and expressive.

In Kotlin, exceptions are objects that inherit from the `Throwable` class. An exception is thrown using the `throw` keyword, and it can be caught and handled within a `try-catch` block.

```
try {
    // Code that might throw an exception
} catch (e: SomeException) {
    // Code to handle the exception
} finally {
    // Optional block that executes regardless of exception occurrence
}
```

The `try` block contains the code that might cause an exception, while the `catch` block defines how to handle the exception if it occurs. The `finally` block, which is optional, contains code that executes whether an exception is thrown or not, often used for cleanup activities such as closing files or releasing resources.

Kotlin also introduces a feature called the try-with-resources statement, known in Kotlin as `use`, which simplifies the process of resource management, ensuring that each resource is closed after its operation is complete.

```
FileInputStream("path/to/file.txt").use { fis ->
    // Use the FileInputStream
}
```

In this example, the `FileInputStream` is automatically closed after the execution of the `use` block, regardless of whether an exception occurred or not, eliminating the need for a `finally` block for resource cleanup.

Kotlin encourages the use of unchecked exceptions (which inherit from `RuntimeException`). Checked exceptions, common in Java, are not present in Kotlin, meaning there is no requirement to catch or declare them. This leads to more readable code and eliminates the boilerplate code often associated with Java's exception handling.

To create custom exceptions, one simply needs to extend the `Exception` class or any of its subclasses.

```
1  class CustomException(message: String): Exception(message)
```

Here, `CustomException` is a new exception type that takes a message as an argument, much like any standard exception in Kotlin.

Lastly, Kotlin supports the use of multiple catch blocks, allowing for more granular exception handling. The catch blocks are evaluated in order, and the first catch block that can handle the thrown exception type will execute. This feature is particularly useful for handling different types of exceptions in a differentiated manner.

```
1  try {
2      // Code that might throw different types of exceptions
3  } catch (e: IOException) {
4      // Handle IOException
5  } catch (e: SQLException) {
6      // Handle SQLException
7  } catch (e: Exception) {
8      // Handle any other Exception
9  }
```

To summarize, Kotlin simplifies exception handling with its syntax and features such as the `use` function for resource management and the removal of checked exceptions. This streamlines error handling in Kotlin, making it straightforward and less prone to error.

3.12   Annotations and Reflection in Kotlin

Annotations in Kotlin are means of attaching metadata to code. This metadata can be read at compile-time or runtime, allowing for more robust and flexible code structures. Kotlin's annotation syntax is straightforward, mirroring its commitment to concise and expressive code.

To define an annotation in Kotlin, one uses the @ symbol followed by the annotation name. Annotations can be applied to classes, functions, properties, parameters, and expressions. Here is a basic example of defining and using an annotation in Kotlin:

```
1  annotation class SpecialFeature(val description: String)
2
3  @SpecialFeature("Very unique functionality")
4  fun uniqueFunction() {
5      println("This function is special.")
6  }
```

In the above example, `SpecialFeature` is an annotation taking a `String` parameter. It is used to annotate `uniqueFunction`, potentially allowing tools or libraries to process that function in a special way.

Reflecting upon Kotlin code enables introspection of these annotations and other code structures at runtime, a powerful feature facilitated through Kotlin's `reflect` library. Reflection is the ability of a program to examine and modify its own structure and behavior at runtime. Kotlin's reflection capabilities allow developers to dynamically access the properties and functions of classes.

To utilize reflection in Kotlin, one must add the `kotlin-reflect` library to their project dependencies. Here is an example of using reflection to access annotations:

```
1  import kotlin.reflect.full.*
2
3  fun main() {
4      val function = ::uniqueFunction
5      val annotations = function.annotations
```

```
6
7    for (annotation in annotations) {
8        println(annotation.annotationClass.simpleName)
9        if (annotation is SpecialFeature) {
10           println("Description: ${annotation.description}")
11       }
12   }
13 }
```

In this example, ::uniqueFunction obtains a reference to the uniqueFunction function, allowing us to introspect its annotations. The annotations property is a list of all annotations applied to the function, which we iterate over to find and process a SpecialFeature annotation.

Furthermore, Kotlin supports various built-in annotations affecting its compile-time behavior, such as @JvmStatic, @JvmOverloads, and @JvmField, which instruct the Kotlin compiler to generate code in specific ways for interoperability with Java.

Finally, Kotlin's reflection API includes the KClass, KCallable, KFunction, KProperty, among others, allowing for comprehensive inspection and interaction with class structures, functions, and properties.

To retrieve a class reference in Kotlin for reflection purposes, use the ::class syntax as shown:

```
1  val kclass = uniqueFunction::class
2  println("Class simple name: ${kclass.simpleName}")
```

This introspective capability, coupled with Kotlin's type-safe design, enables developers to write dynamic, robust applications and libraries that can leverage the full expressiveness and flexibility of the Kotlin language.

Chapter 4

Functions in Kotlin

Diving deeper into Kotlin's capabilities, this chapter focuses on functions, a cornerstone of the Kotlin programming language that facilitates modular, readable, and reusable code. It explores the declaration and use of functions, including concepts such as default and named parameters, vararg parameters, extension functions, and higher-order functions. The chapter also discusses the strategic use of inline functions to optimize performance and demonstrates how Kotlin's support for functional programming can elegantly solve complex problems. Through practical examples, readers will learn to harness the power of functions in Kotlin to write expressive and efficient applications.

4.1 Defining and Calling Functions

Kotlin functions are defined using the fun keyword, followed by the function name, parameters enclosed in parentheses, and the return type. The basic syntax for defining a function is as follows:

```
fun functionName(param1: Type1, param2: Type2, ...): ReturnType {
    // function body
}
```

Each parameter in the function definition is specified by its name followed by a colon and its type. The return type of the function is also specified after the parameters list, preceded by a colon. If a function does not return any value, its return type is Unit, which is similar to void in other programming languages. However, specifying Unit is optional.

Let's start with a simple example.   The following function, addNumbers, takes two integers as input and returns their sum:

```
1   fun addNumbers(a: Int, b: Int): Int {
2       return a + b
3   }
```

To call a function, write the function name followed by the arguments in parentheses. The following demonstrates calling the addNumbers function with arguments 5 and 3:

```
1   val result = addNumbers(5, 3)
```

The result variable will hold the value returned by addNumbers, which in this case is 8.

```
Output:
8
```

Kotlin also allows defining functions with default parameter values. If the caller omits such parameters, the default values are used:

```
1   fun greet(name: String, msg: String = "Hello") {
2       println("$msg $name")
3   }
```

In this example, calling greet with both parameters will print a personalized greeting:

```
1   greet("Alice", "Hi")
```

```
Output:
Hi Alice
```

However, calling greet with only the name will still result in a greeting, thanks to the default message:

94

```
1  greet("Bob")
```

```
Output:
Hello Bob
```

In summary, Kotlin's function syntax is designed to be clean and concise, with support for default parameters increasing its flexibility. The ability to define and call functions with minimal boilerplate code enhances Kotlin's appeal for developing modern software applications.

4.2 Function Parameters and Return Types

In Kotlin, functions are first-class citizens, embodying the principle that code should be concise, readable, and efficient. This section will elucidate the syntax and semantics of function parameters and return types, which are fundamental to defining and invoking functions in Kotlin.

Defining Function Parameters

Function parameters in Kotlin are defined within the parentheses that follow the function name. Each parameter specification includes a name followed by a colon and its type. Here is a basic example of a function that takes two integers and prints their sum:

```
1  fun add(a: Int, b: Int) {
2      println(a + b)
3  }
```

When calling this function, you must provide two arguments of type Int. The parameters a and b are accessible within the function body.

Specifying Return Types

In Kotlin, every function declares the type of value it returns. A function that does not return a value explicitly has the return type Unit, which can be omitted. For functions returning a value, the return type is specified after the parameter list, separated by a colon. Consider the following function that returns the sum of two integers:

```
1  fun add(a: Int, b: Int): Int {
2    return a + b
3  }
```

Here, Int after the colon indicates that add returns an integer value. The return keyword is used to return the result.

Optional Parameters and Default Values

Kotlin supports default values for function parameters, allowing you to call a function with fewer arguments than defined. Specify the default value with an equals sign after the type declaration. Here's how you could modify the add function to have a default value for the second parameter:

```
1  fun add(a: Int, b: Int = 0): Int {
2    return a + b
3  }
```

With this definition, you can call add with either one or two arguments. If the second argument is omitted, Kotlin uses the default value of 0.

Function Calls and Argument Passing

To call a function, use the function name followed by parentheses enclosing the arguments. If the function requires multiple arguments, separate them with commas. For instance, to call the previously defined add function with two numbers:

```
1  val result = add(5, 3)
```

```
Output: 8
```

To leverage default argument values, you may omit arguments from the end of the argument list, or use named arguments for clarity or to specify them out of order. For example:

```
1  val sumOne = add(5)
2  val sumTwo = add(b = 3, a = 2)
```

Named arguments are especially useful when a function has multiple parameters of the same type or when using boolean arguments, as they make the function calls more readable.

Function parameters and return types are the backbone of Kotlin's function definition syntax. Properly using parameters, specifying return types, and understanding how to call functions with arguments, are crucial skills for any Kotlin programmer. This capability promotes code reusability, readability, and maintainability, adhering to Kotlin's philosophy of pragmatism and conciseness. The following sections will build upon these foundational concepts, demonstrating the power and flexibility of functions in Kotlin.

4.3 Default and Named Arguments

In this section, we will discuss the functionalities and advantages of Kotlin's default and named arguments in function declarations and calls. Kotlin provides a way to define functions with default values for parameters, allowing for more concise and flexible function invocations. Additionally, named arguments can be used to improve the readability of function calls, especially when dealing with multiple parameters or default values.

Default Arguments

In Kotlin, you can specify default values for function parameters. This feature enables you to call a function without explicitly passing arguments for every parameter, as long as a default value is provided. To define a function with default arguments, you simply assign values to parameters in the function declaration.

Consider the following example, which defines a function that formats a greeting message:

```
1  fun greetMessage(name: String, greeting: String = "Hello"): String {
2      return "$greeting, $name!"
3  }
```

In this example, the parameter `greeting` has a default value of "Hello". Thus, the function can be called with just the `name` parameter, and the default value for `greeting` will be used:

```
1  val message = greetMessage("Kotlin User")
2  println(message) // Output will be "Hello, Kotlin User!"
```

However, if you wish to use a different greeting, you can explicitly pass both parameters:

```
1  val anotherMessage = greetMessage("Kotlin User", "Welcome")
2  println(anotherMessage) // Output will be "Welcome, Kotlin User!"
```

Named Arguments

Named arguments allow you to specify the values for parameters by name, rather than by position. This feature is particularly useful when a function has a large number of parameters, or when you want to specify only certain parameters with non-default values.

To use named arguments, simply specify the parameter name followed by an equals sign and the value when calling a function:

```
1  val message = greetMessage(name = "Kotlin Developer", greeting = "Hi")
2  println(message) // Output will be "Hi, Kotlin Developer!"
```

Named arguments can be combined with default argument values, allowing you to only override specific parameters:

```
1  val namedMessage = greetMessage(name = "Kotlin Enthusiast")
2  println(namedMessage) // Output will be "Hello, Kotlin Enthusiast!"
```

Named arguments provide several benefits:

- Improve the readability of function calls by making it clear what each argument represents.

- Allow for a flexible order of arguments, making the function calls more intuitive.

- Enable the selective overriding of default parameter values without affecting others.

To summarize, default and named arguments are powerful features of Kotlin that contribute to the language's expressiveness and flexibility. By allowing the omission of arguments that have sensible defaults and specifying arguments by name rather than position, Kotlin functions become more versatile and their calls more readable.

4.4 Using vararg Parameters

Kotlin introduces a flexible approach to handling a function that accepts an arbitrary number of arguments through the vararg keyword. This feature is particularly useful when the exact number of inputs the function will operate on is not known at compile time. The vararg parameters allow for zero or more values of a specified type to be passed to the function, thus providing the versatility needed in various programming scenarios.

Consider a function calculateSum designed to accept an unspecified number of integer values and return their sum. Without the vararg keyword, accommodating an arbitrary number of arguments would be cumbersome, often requiring the use of an array or a list as a parameter, which, in turn, complicates the function call. With vararg, the implementation is straightforward:

```kotlin
fun calculateSum(vararg numbers: Int): Int {
    var sum = 0
    for (number in numbers) {
        sum += number
    }
    return sum
}
```

To call this function, you can pass any number of Int arguments:

```kotlin
val sum = calculateSum(1, 2, 3, 4, 5)
println(sum)
```

The function calculateSum iterates through the numbers array internally created by the vararg keyword and accumulates their sum. The output of the previous call would be:

```
15
```

It demonstrates the function effectively managing five integer inputs without requiring any additional arrays or lists from the caller.

A notable aspect of the vararg keyword is its compatibility with other parameters. When using vararg alongside fixed parameters, it is essential to position the vararg parameter at the end. This placement ensures unambiguous function calls. Here is an example:

```kotlin
fun printNames(message: String, vararg names: String) {
    println(message)
    names.forEach { name ->
        println(name)
    }
}
```

You can invoke the above function as follows:

```kotlin
printNames("These are your students:", "John", "Doe", "Jane")
```

This flexibility is powerful, allowing for a mix of fixed and variable argument lengths within a single function declaration.

Further extending the utility of vararg, Kotlin provides the spread operator (*). This operator allows you to pass an array to a vararg parameter as if each element of the array were being passed as a separate argument:

```
1  val numbersArray = intArrayOf(1, 2, 3, 4, 5)
2  val sum = calculateSum(*numbersArray)
3  println(sum)
```

This feature is particularly handy when the arguments to be passed to the `vararg` parameter are already collected into an array.

The `vararg` parameter in Kotlin offers a flexible and concise means to handle functions that can take a variable number of arguments. This flexibility, combined with the ability to mix `vararg` parameters with fixed parameters and the utility of the `spread` operator, makes `vararg` a powerful feature for Kotlin developers. Whether creating utility functions, aggregating data, or simply needing to pass an unspecified number of values, `vararg` parameters streamline the process, resulting in cleaner, more readable code.

4.5   Extension Functions and Properties

Extension functions and properties allow us to add new functionalities to existing classes without inheriting from them. In Kotlin, this feature provides a powerful mechanism to extend the capabilities of classes even if we do not have access to their source code. This section will elucidate how to declare and utilize extension functions and properties, along with how they work under the hood, enhancing the capability to write more concise and expressive code.

To declare an extension function, prefix the name of the class to be extended to the function name. This does not modify the original class, but it allows the function to be called as if it were a method of that class. Consider extending the class `String` to check if it is a valid email address.

```
1  fun String.isValidEmail(): Boolean {
2      return this.contains("@") && this.contains(".")
3  }
```

Following this declaration, we can now call `isValidEmail()` on any `String` instance as if `String` originally had it.

```
1  val email = "example@example.com"
2  println(email.isValidEmail())
```

```
true
```

Similarly, extension properties can be defined to add new properties to existing classes. They are declared like regular properties but with a class name prefix. However, since extension properties cannot actually insert new data into an object, they must be defined through either a getter or a setter.

```
1  val String.domain: String
2      get() = substringAfterLast('@')
```

Using the above extension property, you can extract the domain of an email address effortlessly.

```
1  val emailDomain = email.domain
2  println(emailDomain)
```

```
example.com
```

It's noteworthy to mention that extension functions and properties are resolved statically, at compile time, and not dynamically, at runtime. This means that the extension function or property to be called is determined by the type of the variable, not by the type of the object that the variable holds at runtime. For instance:

```
1  open class A
2
3  class B: A()
4
5  fun A.extensionFunction() = "A"
6  fun B.extensionFunction() = "B"
7
8  fun printExtensionFunction(a: A) {
9      println(a.extensionFunction())
10 }
11
```

```
12   val a: A = B()
13   printExtensionFunction(a)
```

A

The output is A since the type of the variable a is A, hence A's extension function is called.

Extension functions and properties can significantly enhance the readability and brevity of Kotlin code. They provide a flexible and powerful tool for developers, enabling them to write clean and concise code by logically grouping functionalities even when extending existing classes. However, it is important to use them judiciously to avoid cluttering classes with too many responsibilities.

4.6 Higher-Order Functions: Passing Functions as Parameters

Higher-order functions refer to functions that can take functions as parameters and/or return functions. In Kotlin, this capability adds a powerful tool to the developer's toolbox, enabling more abstract, flexible, and readable code. Utilizing higher-order functions can significantly streamline operations that would otherwise require verbose and repetitive code. This section will cover the syntax and usage of higher-order functions in Kotlin, providing clear examples to illustrate their benefits.

First, let's consider the syntax for declaring a higher-order function. A function that takes another function as a parameter is declared by specifying that parameter's type as a function type. Function types are represented by using the types of the parameters and the return value, enclosed in parentheses, followed by an arrow, and then the return type of the function. Here's a general structure:

```
1   fun <NameOfFunction>(<paramName>: (<ParamTypes>) -> <ReturnType>) {
2       // function body
3   }
```

103

To demonstrate, imagine a simple scenario where we want to apply
a transformation to an integer value. This transformation will be defined by the function passed as a parameter:

```
1  fun transform(value: Int, operation: (Int) -> Int): Int {
2      return operation(value)
3  }
```

In the above example, transform is a higher-order function accepting an integer and a function that itself takes an integer parameter
and returns an integer. The transformation is applied through the
invocation of operation(value).

To use this higher-order function, a compatible function must be provided as an argument. Here is how it can be done:

```
1  val result = transform(5, { x -> x * 2 })
```

The output, stored in result, would be 10. The lambda expression
{ x -> x * 2 } is passed to transform function and applied to the
value 5.

Kotlin also supports passing named functions as arguments to
higher-order functions. Given a function double, defined as follows:

```
1  fun double(x: Int): Int = x * 2
```

It can be passed to the transform function like so:

```
1  val result = transform(10, ::double)
```

In this case, ::double is a reference to the double function, and
result would hold the value 20.

Higher-order functions are not limited to taking single functions as
parameters. They can accept multiple functions, functions with
multiple parameters, and even functions that return other functions.
This flexibility allows developers to construct complex logic in an
elegant, readable, and reusable way. For example, a higher-order
function that applies two operations sequentially could be
represented as follows:

```
1  fun applyOperations(value: Int, operation1: (Int) -> Int, operation2:
```

104

```
      (Int) -> Int): Int {
2       val result1 = operation1(value)
3       return operation2(result1)
4 }
```

This functional-oriented approach to coding provides a succinct and expressive means of solving problems. Through the use of higher-order functions, Kotlin encourages writing code that is not only effective but also clean and concise.

4.7 Lambda Expressions and Anonymous Functions

Lambda expressions and anonymous functions are pivotal in Kotlin for incorporating functional programming paradigms. Both allow for the concise creation of functions that can be passed as arguments, returned as values, or stored in variables. This section elucidates their syntax, differences, and practical use cases.

Lambda Expressions

Lambda expressions in Kotlin are essentially unnamed function blocks that can be passed immediately as an expression. Defined by curly braces {}, lambda expressions can take parameters, body, and return values. The syntax for a lambda expression is shown below:

```
1 val sum = { a: Int, b: Int -> a + b }
```

Here, sum is a variable holding a lambda function that accepts two integers and returns their sum. Parameters are defined within the opening curly brace, followed by the '->' symbol, which separates the parameter list from the lambda body.

Lambda expressions become powerful when used in conjunction with higher-order functions—functions that accept functions as parameters. Consider the following example using Kotlin's `filter` function:

```
1  val numbers = listOf(1, 2, 3, 4, 5)
2  val evenNumbers = numbers.filter { it % 2 == 0 }
```

In this example, `filter` expects a lambda that defines a criteria. `it` is an implicit name for a single parameter in the lambda. The lambda returns `true` for even numbers, thereby filtering the list.

Anonymous Functions

While similar to lambda expressions, anonymous functions offer a more explicit syntax that allows for direct specification of the return type. The syntax for an anonymous function is:

```
1  val sum: (Int, Int) -> Int = fun(a: Int, b: Int): Int { return a + b }
```

Here, `sum` is an anonymous function with specified input and return types. Unlike lambda expressions, anonymous functions use the `fun` keyword and allow for an explicit `return` statement.

Anonymous functions become useful when dealing with complex functions where the type inference system may not easily derive the type, or when a more expressive syntax is preferred for clarity.

Differences and Use Cases

While lambda expressions and anonymous functions can often be used interchangeably in Kotlin, there are slight differences that may make one more suitable than the other in certain contexts:

- **Syntax and Conciseness:** Lambda expressions tend to be more concise and are thus preferred for short, simple functions or when used as arguments to higher-order functions.

- **Return Types:** Anonymous functions allow for the explicit declaration of return types, which can enhance clarity, particularly in complex functions.

106

- **Return Behavior:** In lambda expressions, the last expression is implicitly returned. In contrast, anonymous functions require an explicit `return` statement, offering more control over the return logic.

To summarize, both lambda expressions and anonymous functions play significant roles in Kotlin's support for functional programming. Choosing between them depends on the specific requirements of the function, such as its complexity, intended use, and the need for explicit type declarations or return statements.

4.8   Inline Functions and Performance

Inline functions in Kotlin are a powerful feature designed to optimize performance by reducing call overhead. When a function is declared as `inline`, the Kotlin compiler copies the function's bytecode into the places where the function is called, rather than actually calling the function. This leads to a reduction in the number of function calls, which can substantially improve the performance of an application, especially in high-frequency areas or tight loops.

To declare an inline function, the `inline` modifier is placed before the `fun` keyword. Consider the following example of an inline function definition:

```
1   inline fun <T> performOperation(value: T, operation: (T) -> Unit) {
2       operation(value)
3   }
```

The `performOperation` function takes a generic value and a function `operation` as parameters. The operation is applied to the value within the function body. By marking this function as `inline`, we instruct the compiler to inline the `operation` at each call site, thereby eliminating the overhead of the function call.

One significant advantage of using inline functions is observed when passing lambda expressions as arguments. Without inlining, a lambda expression would result in the creation of an anonymous class, adding to the runtime overhead. However, with an inline function, this overhead is virtually eliminated, as the code for the lambda gets inlined along with the function itself.

It's important to note, however, that inlining large functions can lead to an increase in bytecode size, which could potentially negate the performance benefits. Thus, it is generally recommended to inline only small functions.

Moreover, inline functions support reified type parameters. This feature allows type checking and casting of generic types at runtime, which is not possible with regular functions due to type erasure. Consider the following example:

```
1  inline fun <reified T> isOfType(value: Any): Boolean = value is T
```

This function checks if the given value is of type T, which is determined at runtime thanks to the reified keyword.

Another aspect to consider is the limitation with respect to non-local returns. In a regular function, returning from a lambda expression simply returns from the lambda itself. However, in an inline function, since the lambda code is inlined, a return statement within a lambda would return from the host function. Although this behavior can be useful for control flow, it must be used with caution to avoid unintended returns from the enclosing function.

Inline functions are a crucial feature in Kotlin for optimizing performance by eliminating the overhead of function calls and enabling advanced features like reified type parameters and non-local returns. However, they should be used judiciously, with consideration for the implications on bytecode size and control flow.

4.9   Tail Recursive Functions

Tail recursion is a specific kind of recursion where the recursive call is the final action in the function. This concept is vital in Kotlin as it allows the compiler to optimize recursive calls to iterative ones, preventing stack overflow errors that typically occur with deep recursion. Kotlin facilitates this through the `tailrec` modifier, which marks a function as tail recursive.

Consider a classic example of calculating the factorial of a number. A straightforward recursive approach might look like this:

```
1  fun factorial(n: Int): Int {
2      return if (n == 1) 1 else n * factorial(n-1)
3  }
```

While this function correctly computes the factorial, it is not tail-recursive because the last operation is a multiplication, not the recursive call itself. For a function to be tail-recursive, the recursive call must be the last action it performs. Rewriting the above function to be tail recursive involves adding an accumulator parameter that carries the computation result through each recursive call:

```
1  tailrec fun factorial(n: Int, acc: Int = 1): Int {
2      return if (n == 1) acc else factorial(n-1, n*acc)
3  }
```

In this revised version, the `tailrec` modifier tells the Kotlin compiler that the function is tail-recursive, which it confirms by ensuring the recursive call is in the tail position – the last action performed. The compiler then optimizes this recursive call to a more performant loop under the hood.

Another common example is computing Fibonacci numbers. A naive recursive implementation can be highly inefficient for large inputs due to the exponential growth of recursive calls. However, by using tail recursion, we can maintain linear performance:

```
1  tailrec fun fibonacci(n: Int, a: Long = 0, b: Long = 1): Long {
2      return if (n == 0) a else fibonacci(n-1, b, a+b)
3  }
```

This function iteratively computes Fibonacci numbers in a manner that's both clear and efficient, thanks to tail recursion optimization.

To illustrate the efficiency and safety of tail recursive functions, let's compare stack usage between a tail recursive implementation and a non-tail recursive one. We can simulate a stack depth measurement by modifying the recursive functions to increment a counter every time the function is called:

```
1   var counter = 0
2
3   fun factorialCounter(n: Int): Int {
4       counter++
5       return if (n == 1) 1 else n * factorialCounter(n-1)
6   }
7
8   fun resetCounter() { counter = 0 }
```

Running the factorialCounter function with a large value of n will result in a StackOverflowError beyond a certain depth, evidencing the limitation of non-tail recursive functions in handling deep recursion. Conversely, the tail-recursive variant will not incur such errors, demonstrating its resilience and efficiency.

The use of tail recursion in Kotlin, enabled by the tailrec modifier, allows developers to write clean, efficient recursive functions without fearing stack overflow errors. This feature is especially useful for algorithms inherently recursive, such as factorial computation, Fibonacci sequence generation, and tree traversal algorithms.

4.10   Operator Overloading and Conventions

In Kotlin, operator overloading is a syntactic feature that allows developers to provide custom implementations for the behavior of operators (such as +, -, *, /) when they are applied to user-defined types. Implemented properly, operator overloading can make code using custom types as intuitive to read and write as code using Kotlin's built-in types.

The Mechanics of Operator Overloading

To overload an operator, Kotlin requires the definition of a function marked with the 'operator' modifier. Each operator has a corresponding function name, for example, the '+' operator corresponds to the function 'plus'. Let's demonstrate this with an example involving a custom class ComplexNumber for complex numbers:

```
1  class ComplexNumber(val real: Double, val imaginary: Double) {
2      operator fun plus(other: ComplexNumber): ComplexNumber {
3          return ComplexNumber(real + other.real, imaginary + other.
               imaginary)
4      }
5  }
```

Here, the ComplexNumber class defines a plus function marked with the 'operator' modifier. You can now use the '+' operator to add two instances of ComplexNumber:

```
1  val number1 = ComplexNumber(1.0, 2.0)
2  val number2 = ComplexNumber(3.0, 4.0)
3  val sum = number1 + number2
```

The use of '+' operator in the example code will internally call the plus method of number1, passing number2 as an argument.

Supported Operators

Kotlin allows overloading a wide range of operators. These include:

- Unary prefix operators like '+' and '-' (correspond to unaryPlus and unaryMinus)

- Binary operators like '*' and '/' (correspond to times and div)

- Assignment operators like '+=' (these do not have corresponding functions; instead, a combination of plus and assignment is used)

111

- Comparison operators like '==' and '<' (correspond to `equals` and `compareTo`)

- Indexed access operator '[]' (corresponds to functions `get` and `set`)

- And many more

Conventions and Restrictions

It is crucial to remember that while operator overloading can make code more intuitive, misuse might lead to confusion and reduced code readability. Thus, adhere to the following conventions and restrictions:

- Overload operators in such a way that their behavior is consistent with their intuitive geometric or algebraic meaning.

- Kotlin does not allow overloading of assignment operators (like "+=" directly) except through providing a corresponding binary operator (like "+").

- The 'equals' operator should always adhere to its contract, which includes consistency, reflexivity, symmetry, and transitivity.

Utilizing Operator Overloading

Implementing operators judiciously can lead to concise and readable code. However, ensure that the overloading aligns with the natural intuition surrounding an operator's use. The design of Kotlin encourages this approach through the restrictions and conventions it imposes on operator overloading.

4.11   Infix Notation for Function Calls

In this section, we will discuss the usage of infix notation for function calls in Kotlin. Infix notation allows for more readable and concise code, particularly when the function acts as an operation between two operands. Kotlin provides the ability to define functions that can be called using infix notation, which means that the function name is placed between the caller (the object) and the parameter.

To declare a function that can be called using infix notation, the `infix` modifier is used. It is important to note that infix functions must satisfy the following conditions:

- They must be member functions or extension functions.

- They must have a single parameter.

- The parameter must not accept variable number of arguments and must have no default value.

The general syntax of an infix function declaration is as follows:

```
infix fun ClassName.functionName(param: ParamType): ReturnType {
    // function body
}
```

Consider the following example where we define a class `Item` with an infix function `isSameAs` that compares two `Item` objects:

```
class Item(val id: Int, val name: String) {
    infix fun isSameAs(other: Item): Boolean {
        return this.id == other.id && this.name == other.name
    }
}

fun main() {
    val item1 = Item(1, "apple")
    val item2 = Item(1, "apple")
    val item3 = Item(2, "banana")

    if (item1 isSameAs item2) {
        println("Item1 is the same as Item2.")
    } else {
```

```
15        println("Item1 is not the same as Item2.")
16    }
17
18    if (item1 isSameAs item3) {
19        println("Item1 is the same as Item3.")
20    } else {
21        println("Item1 is not the same as Item3.")
22    }
23 }
```

The output of the program is:

```
Item1 is the same as Item2.
Item1 is not the same as Item3.
```

This example illustrates how infix notation contributes to the readability of the code, making it look more like natural language. The infix function isSameAs is called on item1 with item2 and item3 as arguments, checking if they are the same.

Infix notation can be particularly useful when designing domain-specific languages (DSLs) or APIs that benefit from syntax that closely resembles natural language, thereby improving clarity and reducing potential for confusion.

Additionally, infix functions can be used with generic types, further enhancing their versatility for different use cases. An example declaration would be:

```
1  infix fun <T> T.isEqualTo(other: T): Boolean {
2      return this == other
3  }
```

As illustrated above, infix notation in Kotlin is a powerful feature that, when used appropriately, can make the code significantly more readable and expressive. It is, however, important to use it judiciously to ensure that the readability of the code is genuinely enhanced and not compromised by overuse.

4.12   Local Functions and Structured Concurrency

In this section, we will discuss an advanced feature of Kotlin that allows for more concise and structured code: local functions. Additionally, we will tie this concept to structured concurrency, a paradigm that significantly simplifies concurrent programming in Kotlin.

Local functions in Kotlin are functions declared within another function. This feature lets developers encapsulate function logic that does not need to be exposed outside the containing function, leading to more modular and easier-to-read code. Here's a basic example of a local function within a Kotlin function:

```
1  fun outerFunction() {
2      fun localFunction() {
3          println("I am a local function")
4      }
5      localFunction()
6  }
```

In this example, localFunction() is only accessible within the scope of outerFunction(). Attempting to call localFunction() outside of outerFunction() would result in a compilation error.

Moreover, local functions can access variables from the outer function, which makes it handy for tasks that require manipulating shared data without exposing that logic publicly:

```
1  fun performCalculations(number: Int) {
2      val initialValue = number
3
4      fun increment() = number + 1
5      fun double() = number * 2
6
7      val incrementedValue = increment()
8      val doubledValue = double()
9
10     println("Initial: $initialValue, Incremented: $incrementedValue,
           Doubled: $doubledValue")
11 }
```

115

Now, let's connect local functions to structured concurrency. Structured concurrency is a concept in Kotlin that simplifies concurrent programming by structuring concurrent operations in a way that ensures they are automatically started and stopped with the lifecycle of a corresponding block of code. This results in more manageable concurrent code and reduces the risk of leaks or unforeseen side effects. Kotlin's coroutines heavily rely on structured concurrency to manage concurrent tasks.

Here is an example demonstrating the use of local functions within a coroutine to perform concurrent tasks:

```
import kotlinx.coroutines.launch
import kotlinx.coroutines.runBlocking

fun main() = runBlocking {
    launch {
        fun log(message: String) {
            println("[${Thread.currentThread().name}] $message")
        }

        log("Task 1 started")
        // Simulate a long-running task
        delay(1000)
        log("Task 1 completed")
    }
    launch {
        fun log(message: String) {
            println("[${Thread.currentThread().name}] $message")
        }

        log("Task 2 started")
        // Simulate another long-running task
        delay(1000)
        log("Task 2 completed")
    }
}
```

In this concurrent programming example, log() is a local function defined inside each coroutine block. It helps in logging messages along with the corresponding thread name, improving the readability and maintainability of the concurrency-related code.

Local functions, when used appropriately, can remarkably reduce the visibility of auxiliary functions that are not meant to be used outside of their containing functions. Coupled with structured concurrency, local functions can also contribute to writing more intuitive and safer concurrent Kotlin code.

Chapter 5

Working with Collections

This chapter delves into Kotlin's comprehensive support for collections, such as lists, sets, and maps, which are fundamental for storing and managing groups of objects. It covers both mutable and immutable collections, providing insights into when and how to use each effectively in applications. Further, the chapter introduces the range of operations available on collections, including filtering, mapping, sorting, and aggregating data. By demonstrating Kotlin's powerful and expressive collection APIs, readers will learn to manipulate collections efficiently, enabling the development of more sophisticated and robust applications.

5.1 Overview of Collections in Kotlin

Kotlin, distinguished by its conciseness and expressive power, offers a well-designed set of collection interfaces and classes that form the backbone of data storage and manipulation in applications. Collections in Kotlin are an evolution from Java collections, optimized for readability and operational efficiency. This section elucidates the core concepts and types of collections available in Kotlin: lists, sets, and maps, and their significance in programming.

Collections are essentially containers of objects; they hold and manage groups of objects, enabling developers to perform a wide array of operations like searching, sorting, filtering, and transformation. Kotlin treats collections primarily as interfaces, permitting a wide variety of implementations while maintaining a consistent API surface. The two major categories of collections in Kotlin are:

- **Read-only collections** - These are collections that only support read operations, such as accessing elements and iterating over them. They map to Kotlin's collection interfaces like `List`, `Set`, and `Map`.

- **Mutable collections** - In contrast to read-only collections, mutable collections provide operations that modify the collection, such as adding, removing, and updating elements. These are represented by interfaces like `MutableList`, `MutableSet`, and `MutableMap`.

Understanding the distinction between mutable and immutable (read-only) collections is crucial for effective Kotlin programming. While immutable collections ensure safety by preventing unintended modifications, mutable collections offer flexibility where modifications are necessary.

The type of collection chosen (list, set, or map) depends on the specific requirements of the application:

- **Lists** (`List` and `MutableList`) - Ordered collections that can contain duplicate elements. They are particularly useful when the order of elements is important and when allowing duplicates.

- **Sets** (`Set` and `MutableSet`) - Collections that contain unique elements. They are the go-to choice when it is necessary to eliminate duplicates and when the order of elements is not significant.

- **Maps** (`Map` and `MutableMap`) - Collections of key-value pairs, where each key is unique. Maps are ideal for lookups by key, where each key maps to a specific value.

Each type of collection offers a wide range of functions to manipulate the data they hold, such as filtering, mapping, aggregation, and sorting. Understanding these operations and how they apply to different types of collections is essential for harnessing the full power of Kotlin collections.

The efficiency of Kotlin collections is further improved through the use of sequences, which offer a lazy collection evaluation, allowing for more performant chaining of operations in some scenarios. Moreover, Kotlin provides a series of collection builders and utility functions, which simplify the instantiation and configuration of complex collections.

In summary, Kotlin collections are a fundamental aspect of the language, designed to provide a rich set of tools for managing groups of objects. By offering both mutable and immutable versions of lists, sets, and maps, Kotlin enables developers to choose the most appropriate type of collection and operations for their specific application needs, ensuring both safety and flexibility in data manipulation.

5.2   Creating Lists, Sets, and Maps

Creating and manipulating collections such as lists, sets, and maps are essential skills in Kotlin programming. These collection types offer powerful ways to store and manage data. Kotlin provides clear and concise methods to create these collections, supporting both mutable and immutable versions. This section provides detailed insights into how to instantiate lists, sets, and maps, and highlights the distinctions between their mutable and immutable versions.

Lists

A list is an ordered collection of elements that can contain duplicates. Kotlin provides two main types of lists - immutable (List) and mutable (`MutableList`).

Immutable Lists

Immutable lists are created with the `listOf()` function. Here is how to create an immutable list of strings:

```
1  val fruits = listOf("Apple", "Banana", "Cherry")
```

Elements in an immutable list cannot be modified after creation. Attempting to add or remove elements from the list will result in a compilation error.

Mutable Lists

Mutable lists can be created using the `mutableListOf()` function. This allows not only accessing elements but also modifying the list by adding, removing, or updating elements:

```
1  val vegetables = mutableListOf("Carrot", "Potato", "Cabbage")
2  vegetables.add("Tomato")
3  vegetables.removeAt(1)
4  vegetables[1] = "Broccoli"
```

After these operations, the `vegetables` list will contain "Carrot", "Broccoli", and "Tomato".

Sets

A set is a collection of unique elements, meaning it does not support duplicates. Like lists, Kotlin offers immutable (`Set`) and mutable (`MutableSet`) versions.

Immutable Sets

Immutable sets are created with the `setOf()` function:

```
1  val numbers = setOf(1, 2, 3, 3, 2)
```

The duplicate elements "3" and "2" will be ignored, and numbers will only contain 1, 2, 3.

Mutable Sets

Mutable sets are instantiated using the mutableSetOf() function, allowing addition and removal of elements:

```
1  val uniqueFruits = mutableSetOf("Apple", "Banana")
2  uniqueFruits.add("Cherry")
3  uniqueFruits.remove("Banana")
```

The uniqueFruits set will now contain "Apple" and "Cherry".

Maps

A map is a collection of key-value pairs, where each key is unique. Maps come in immutable (Map) and mutable (MutableMap) forms.

Immutable Maps

Immutable maps are created using the mapOf() function. Keys and values are paired using the to keyword:

```
1  val countryCode = mapOf("USA" to "1", "India" to "91", "Germany" to "
       49")
```

Mutable Maps

Mutable maps can be instantiated with the mutableMapOf() function. This permits the addition, removal, and modification of key-value pairs:

```
1  val domainTld = mutableMapOf("com" to "Commercial", "org" to "
       Organization")
2  domainTld.put("net", "Network")
3  domainTld.remove("org")
```

After these operations, the domainTld map will contain mappings for "com" to "Commercial" and "net" to "Network".

In summary, Kotlin offers developers comprehensive support for creating and manipulating collections through its expressive APIs for lists, sets, and maps, both in mutable and immutable forms. Understanding these concepts is fundamental for effective data management in Kotlin applications.

5.3 Mutable vs Immutable Collections

Kotlin distinguishes between mutable and immutable collections to ensure that developers have full control over their data structures, enabling more secure and predictable programming patterns. Understanding the difference between these two types of collections and when to use each is crucial for effective application development in Kotlin.

Immutable Collections

Immutable collections, as the name suggests, are collections whose elements cannot be modified after their creation. Attempting to change the contents of an immutable collection will result in a compilation error. Immutable collections are typically used in situations where a consistent, unchangeable set of data is required.

Kotlin provides immutable versions of the basic collection types: List, Set, and Map. To create an immutable collection, one can use functions such as listOf(), setOf(), and mapOf(). Here is an example demonstrating the creation of an immutable list:

```
1  val immutableList = listOf("Apple", "Banana", "Cherry")
```

Attempting to modify this list, for example by adding or removing elements, will result in a compile-time error. This enforceability makes immutable collections a reliable choice for passing data between components without the concern of unintended modifications.

Mutable Collections

Contrastingly, mutable collections are designed to allow their contents to be modified, including adding, removing, or updating elements after they have been created. Kotlin offers mutable variants of the basic collection types, which include MutableList, MutableSet, and MutableMap. These are created using functions such as mutableListOf(), mutableSetOf(), and mutableMapOf(). Here is how you can create a mutable list:

```
1  val mutableList = mutableListOf("Apple", "Banana", "Cherry")
2  mutableList.add("Date") // This operation is allowed on mutable lists.
```

One of the key advantages of mutable collections is their flexibility. They are particularly useful when dealing with a dataset that is expected to change over time, such as user-generated content or real-time data processing.

Choosing Between Mutable and Immutable Collections

The choice between mutable and immutable collections depends on the specific requirements of the application. Immutable collections offer simplicity and safety, making them a good default choice for most scenarios. However, if performance is a concern, especially in situations involving large datasets or frequent modifications, mutable collections may be more appropriate.

It is also worth mentioning that converting between mutable and immutable collections is straightforward in Kotlin. For instance, to convert a mutable list to an immutable list:

```
1  val immutableList: List<String> = mutableList.toList()
```

This versatility underscores Kotlin's flexibility, allowing developers to choose the most suitable type of collection for their needs while maintaining code readability and safety.

In summary, Kotlin's collection framework is designed with both safety and flexibility in mind, offering developers the choice between mutable and immutable types based on the requirements of their applications. By understanding the characteristics and appropriate use cases for each, developers can harness the power of Kotlin to create more robust and reliable applications.

5.4   Accessing Elements in Collections

In Kotlin, collections such as lists, sets, and maps are not just containers for storing objects but are fundamental constructs that offer a wide range of functionality for efficient data manipulation. Among the most basic yet crucial operations one can perform on collections is accessing their elements. This section focuses on the various methods Kotlin provides for accessing elements in lists, sets, and maps, drawing attention to the unique characteristics of each collection type.

Accessing Elements in Lists: Lists in Kotlin are ordered collections with elements that can be accessed by their index. The index of the first element is 0, incrementing by 1 for each subsequent element. To retrieve an element at a specific index, use the get(index) function or the shorthand list[index] notation.

```
1  val fruits = listOf("Apple", "Banana", "Cherry")
2  val firstFruit = fruits[0] // Accesses "Apple"
3  val secondFruit = fruits.get(1) // Accesses "Banana"
```

It's worth noting that accessing an index outside the bounds of the list will throw an IndexOutOfBoundsException. Hence, ensuring that the index is within the range of 0 to list.size - 1 is crucial.

Kotlin also offers safe ways to access elements that might be out of bounds through methods like getOrElse and getOrNull:

```
1  val safeElement = fruits.getOrNull(3) // Returns null, as index 3 is
       out of bounds
2  val defaultElement = fruits.getOrElse(3) { "Unknown" } // Returns "
```

```
Unknown"
```

Accessing Elements in Sets: Sets are collections that guarantee unique elements and do not support accessing elements by index. However, one can iterate over a set using loops or retrieve specific elements when the order is not a priority:

```
1  val numberSet = setOf(1, 2, 3)
2  for (number in numberSet) {
3      println(number)
4  }
```

Accessing Elements in Maps: Maps store key-value pairs and provide a very efficient way to access values by their keys. To access a value, use the get(key) function or the shorthand map[key] notation. If the key does not exist, both methods will return null.

```
1  val capitalCities = mapOf("France" to "Paris", "Germany" to "Berlin")
2  val capitalOfFrance = capitalCities["France"] // Accesses "Paris"
3  val capitalOfSpain = capitalCities.get("Spain") // Returns null
```

Kotlin also introduces the getOrElse and getOrDefault functions for maps, providing a default value instead of null when the key is not found:

```
1  val capitalOfSpain = capitalCities.getOrDefault("Spain", "Unknown") //
     Returns "Unknown"
```

- Use list[index] or get(index) for lists to access elements by index.

- Iterate over sets as they do not support index-based access.

- Use map[key] or get(key) for maps to access values by key.

- Employ getOrDefault and getOrElse to safely access elements without encountering exceptions.

Understanding how to access elements in collections is indispensable for effectively manipulating data. As Kotlin collection APIs are designed to abstract away much of the complexity, they enable developers to focus more on implementing logic rather than managing underlying data structures.

5.5   Collection Operations: Filtering and Mapping

Kotlin offers a plethora of operations for performing computations and transformations on collections.   Among these, filtering and mapping are two pivotal operations that allow developers to process collections in a highly efficient and concise manner.   This section explores these operations in detail, illustrating their usage with practical examples.

Filtering Collections

Filtering is a process that selects elements from a collection that satisfy a particular condition, returning a new collection containing these elements. In Kotlin, this is achieved using the `filter` function. The `filter` function takes a predicate—a lambda expression that returns a Boolean value—determining whether an element should be included in the result.

```
1  val numbers = listOf(1, 2, 3, 4, 5, 6)
2  val evenNumbers = numbers.filter { it % 2 == 0 }
3  println(evenNumbers)
```

```
[2, 4, 6]
```

In this example, the `filter` function is applied to a list of integers, selecting only the even numbers. The predicate `{ it % 2 == 0 }` is applied to each element in the list, and only those for which the predicate returns true are included in the resulting list.

Mapping Collections

Mapping is an operation that transforms each element in a collection according to a specified function, producing a new collection of the transformed elements. This is accomplished in Kotlin using the map function. The map function applies a transformation function to each element in the original collection and collects the results in a new collection.

```
1  val numbers = listOf(1, 2, 3, 4, 5)
2  val squaredNumbers = numbers.map { it * it }
3  println(squaredNumbers)
```

```
[1, 4, 9, 16, 25]
```

Here, the map function is used to square each number in the original list. The lambda expression { it * it } is the transformation function, taking each element as input and returning its square. The resulting collection contains the squares of the original numbers.

Combining Filtering and Mapping

Filtering and mapping operations can be combined to perform more complex transformations and computations succinctly. The result of a filter operation can be the input to a map operation, or vice versa, depending on the requirements.

```
1  val numbers = listOf(1, 2, 3, 4, 5, 6, 7, 8, 9, 10)
2  val results = numbers.filter { it % 2 == 0 }.map { it * it }
3  println(results)
```

```
[4, 16, 36, 64, 100]
```

In this example, the list of numbers is first filtered to select only the even numbers, then each selected number is squared. This combination allows for powerful and expressive data processing with minimal code.

129

To conclude, Kotlin's filtering and mapping operations provide developers with robust tools for processing collections. By understanding and utilizing these operations, developers can write more expressive, efficient, and maintainable code.

5.6 Aggregating Collection Data

Aggregate operations in Kotlin enable the accumulation of collection data into a single result. This section emphasizes the use of these operations to calculate sums, averages, or custom accumulations by employing functions such as sum(), average(), fold(), and reduce().

Sum and Average

Calculating the sum or average of numerical collections is a common requirement. Kotlin simplifies this with the sum() and average() functions.

```
val numbers = listOf(1, 2, 3, 4, 5)
val sum = numbers.sum()
val average = numbers.average()

println("Sum: $sum")
println("Average: $average")
```

The expected output for this code snippet is:

```
Sum: 15
Average: 3.0
```

Fold and Reduce

While sum() and average() are useful, Kotlin provides more generalized functions for accumulation: fold() and reduce(). Both iterate through the collection, applying an operation on elements. The difference lies in fold() taking an initial value, whereas reduce() uses the first element of the collection as the initial accumulator.

```
1   val numbers = listOf(1, 2, 3, 4, 5)
2
3   // Using `fold` with an initial value of 0
4   val foldedResult = numbers.fold(0) { acc, i -> acc + i }
5
6   // Using `reduce` to sum the numbers without an initial value
7   val reducedResult = numbers.reduce { acc, i -> acc + i }
8
9   println("Folded Sum: $foldedResult")
10  println("Reduced Sum: $reducedResult")
```

Both functions will produce the same sum:

```
Folded Sum: 15
Reduced Sum: 15
```

However, fold() offers greater flexibility due to its ability to specify an initial value. This is particularly useful when the collection might be empty or when starting the accumulation from a non-zero baseline.

Custom Accumulation

Beyond simple arithmetic operations, Kotlin's fold() and reduce() are capable of performing complex aggregations. For instance, to concatenate strings or merge data structures.

```
1   val words = listOf("Kotlin", "is", "fun")
2
3   val concatenated = words.reduce { acc, s -> "$acc $s" }
4
5   println("Concatenated: $concatenated")
```

This results in:

```
Concatenated: Kotlin is fun
```

Optimizations with Laziness

Remember, reduce() and fold() iterate through every element in the collection. In performance-sensitive applications, especially with large collections, consider converting the collection into a sequence to leverage lazy evaluation. Sequences perform operations one element at a time, potentially reducing computational overhead.

```
val largeNumbers = (1..1_000_000).toList()

val sumOfEvenNumbers = largeNumbers
    .asSequence()
    .filter { it % 2 == 0 }
    .reduce { acc, i -> acc + i }

println("Sum of even numbers: $sumOfEvenNumbers")
```

Converting to a sequence before applying filter and reduce limits the number of operations performed, enhancing efficiency by only processing the elements necessary for the final result.

In summary, Kotlin's aggregation functions provide powerful tools for summarizing and transforming collection data. By understanding and applying sum, average, fold, and reduce, developers can implement complex data processing logic succinctly and efficiently.

5.7   Sorting Collections

Sorting is a fundamental operation on collections that organizes elements into a specified order, generally either ascending or descending. Kotlin provides a rich set of functions to facilitate various sorting mechanisms for both mutable and immutable collections. These functions allow easy manipulation and ordering of collection elements based on natural order or a custom-defined order.

To sort a collection in Kotlin, the simplest approach is to use the sorted() function, which returns a new list with elements sorted in ascending order. For instance, sorting a list of integers or strings can be achieved as follows:

```
val numbers = listOf(5, 2, 9, 3, 7)
val sortedNumbers = numbers.sorted()
println(sortedNumbers) // Output: [2, 3, 5, 7, 9]
```

```
5   val words = listOf("banana", "apple", "kiwi")
6   val sortedWords = words.sorted()
7   println(sortedWords) // Output: [apple, banana, kiwi]
```

For sorting objects in a collection based on a specific property, Kotlin offers the `sortedBy` function. This enables sorting elements according to the natural order of the property's value:

```
1   data class Fruit(val name: String, val weight: Int)
2
3   val fruits = listOf(Fruit("banana", 120), Fruit("apple", 100), Fruit("
        kiwi", 80))
4   val sortedFruitsByWeight = fruits.sortedBy { it.weight }
5   println(sortedFruitsByWeight)
```

To sort a collection in descending order, the `sortedDescending()` and `sortedByDescending()` functions are used. These functions work similarly to `sorted()` and `sortedBy()` but invert the order of the elements:

```
1   val descendingNumbers = numbers.sortedDescending()
2   println(descendingNumbers) // Output: [9, 7, 5, 3, 2]
3
4   val sortedFruitsByWeightDesc = fruits.sortedByDescending { it.weight }
5   println(sortedFruitsByWeightDesc)
```

In the case of mutable collections, Kotlin provides the `sort()`, `sortBy()`, `sortDescending()`, and `sortByDescending()` functions, which modify the collection in-place:

```
1   val mutableNumbers = mutableListOf(5, 2, 9, 3, 7)
2   mutableNumbers.sort()
3   println(mutableNumbers) // Output: [2, 3, 5, 7, 9]
4
5   mutableNumbers.sortDescending()
6   println(mutableNumbers) // Output: [9, 7, 5, 3, 2]
```

When the default sorting behavior is not sufficient, and a more complex comparison logic is needed, Kotlin provides the `sortedWith()` function. This function accepts a `Comparator` as an argument, allowing for flexible sorting based on multiple criteria:

```
1   val customSort = fruits.sortedWith(compareByDescending<Fruit> { it.
        weight }.thenBy { it.name })
```

133

```
2   println(customSort)
```

Kotlin's collection sorting mechanisms are comprehensive and versatile, tailored to accommodate a wide range of use cases from simple to complex sorting logic. By understanding and leveraging these sorting functions, developers can implement efficient data organization and retrieval operations in their applications, enhancing their functionality and user experience.

5.8   Sequences and Lazy Evaluation

Kotlin sequences offer a lazy way to do computations on collections. This means that computation on a sequence occurs only when it is necessary and in a step-wise fashion. This feature can be especially beneficial when working with large datasets or when performing complex chains of collection transformations.

- Sequence is created from a collection or a range using the .asSequence() method.

- Operations on a Sequence are divided into intermediate and terminal operations. Intermediate operations return another sequence, while terminal operations return a result or perform an action.

- Sequences provide improved performance over eager evaluation in certain scenarios, especially when dealing with large collections or performing operations that filter elements.

Consider the code snippet below, which demonstrates the creation of a sequence and applying a chain of operations:

```
1   val numbersSequence = listOf(1, 2, 3, 4, 5).asSequence()
2       .map { it * it }
3       .filter { it > 10 }
4
5   println(numbersSequence.toList())
```

The output of the above code snippet is:

```
[16, 25]
```

Notice how the sequence operations are invoked. Initially, numbersSequence is not evaluated. Only when the terminal operation .toList() is called does the computation happen. Each element is squared and then passed to the filter, one element at a time. This chain of operations is highly efficient for two main reasons:

- Each element is processed individually from the start of the pipeline to the end before moving to the next element, minimizing the intermediate memory footprint.

- Computation is deferred until the terminal operation. If a sequence is filtered before being transformed, unnecessary computations are avoided on the elements that are filtered out.

Eager vs Lazy Evaluation: To understand the efficiency of lazy evaluation, consider the same operations applied eagerly to a list:

```
1  val numbersList = listOf(1, 2, 3, 4, 5)
2      .map { it * it }
3      .filter { it > 10 }
4
5  println(numbersList)
```

In the eager evaluation, all elements are first squared, resulting in a temporary intermediate list, and then this list is filtered. This contrasts with lazy evaluation, where computation is done in a streamlined manner without creating unnecessary intermediate collections.

Limitations: While sequence operations are powerful, they come with certain limitations. Not all operations are as efficient when performed on a sequence versus a list. For example, operations that require indexing or the size of the collection are not recommended on sequences due to their inherent nature of sequential processing.

Sequences and their lazy evaluation strategy are powerful tools in Kotlin's collection processing arsenal, optimizing performance and

reducing memory overhead for large collections or complex computation chains. Understanding when and how to use sequences can
significantly improve the efficiency of Kotlin applications.

5.9   Using Collection Builders

Kotlin provides a unique and powerful feature known as collection
builders, which allows for more fluent and expressive instantiation
and population of collections. Among these builders, the 'listOf',
'mutableListOf',   'setOf',   'mutableSetOf',   'mapOf',   and
'mutableMapOf' functions are particularly notable. This section will
discuss the utilization of these functions, demonstrating their
advantages in simplifying collection management.

Immutable Collections

Immutable collections are those that, once created, cannot be
modified.   This means that their size and elements cannot be
changed.   Kotlin encourages the use of immutable collections to
write safer, more predictable code.

```
val immutableList = listOf(1, 2, 3)
val immutableSet = setOf("a", "b", "c")
val immutableMap = mapOf("key1" to 1, "key2" to 2)
```

The 'listOf', 'setOf', and 'mapOf' functions instantiate immutable collections of type List, Set, and Map respectively. These collections can
be iterated, accessed by index (in the case of List), or accessed by key
(in the case of Map), but elements cannot be added or removed.

Mutable Collections

For scenarios where collection content needs to be dynamic, mutable collections are utilized. Mutable collections allow for addition,
removal, and modification of elements post-instantiation. Kotlin pro-

vides 'mutableListOf', 'mutableSetOf', and 'mutableMapOf' for creating mutable versions of lists, sets, and maps.

```
1  val mutableList = mutableListOf(1, 2, 3)
2  val mutableSet = mutableSetOf("a", "b", "c")
3  val mutableMap = mutableMapOf("key1" to 1, "key2" to 2)
```

These collections return instances of `MutableList`, `MutableSet`, and `MutableMap` respectively, each of which provides methods to modify the collection.

Using Collection Builders Effectively

To utilize collection builders effectively, it is important to understand the specific requirements of the application and the characteristics of the data being managed. Immutable collections are preferred for fixed-size data sets or where data integrity is crucial, as they are inherently thread-safe and less prone to errors. Mutable collections are suited for dynamic data sets where elements need to be added, removed, or updated frequently.

One of the benefits of collection builders is their expressive syntax, which supports not only collection instantiation but also inline definition of elements. This can significantly reduce boilerplate code, making programs more concise and readable. Moreover, collection builders seamlessly integrate with Kotlin's functional features, such as lambda expressions, enabling powerful operations like transformation and filtering during collection initialization.

```
1  val squaredNumbers = mutableListOf<Int>().apply {
2      (1..10).forEach { add(it * it) }
3  }
```

In the example above, a mutable list of squared numbers is created using the `apply` function, demonstrating the synergy between collection builders and Kotlin's functional capabilities.

In summary, Kotlin's collection builders offer a versatile and expressive means of working with collections. By selecting the appropriate collection type and leveraging Kotlin's functional features, developers can manipulate collections more efficiently and write cleaner, more intuitive code. Understanding when and how to use these builders is fundamental to effective Kotlin programming, especially in contexts where data manipulation and management are central.

5.10   Working with Ranges and Progressions

Kotlin's support for ranges and progressions is a powerful feature that simplifies the process of working with a series of numbers or characters. This mechanism is highly useful in loops, enabling iteration over a range of values with minimal syntax. This section will provide a comprehensive understanding of how to define and utilize ranges and progressions in Kotlin programming.

Ranges in Kotlin are defined using the '..' operator. The basic form of a range is between two values, where the start value is inclusive, and the end value is also inclusive. Here is an example of defining a range of integers from 1 to 5:

```
val range: IntRange = 1..5
```

Once a range is defined, you can iterate over its values using a for loop:

```
for (i in range) {
    println(i)
}
```

This results in the output:

```
1
2
3
4
5
```

Kotlin provides ranges not only for integers but also for other numeric types and characters. For example, to define a range of characters from 'a' to 'e':

```
1  val charRange: CharRange = 'a'..'e'
```

And to iterate over this range:

```
1  for (char in charRange) {
2      println(char)
3  }
```

Which prints out:

```
a
b
c
d
e
```

Progressions allow more flexibility than ranges because they enable you to define not only the start and end points but also the step by which to iterate. Kotlin uses the `step` function for creating progressions. An example of a progression where we want to iterate from 1 to 10, with a step of 2, is:

```
1  val progression: IntProgression = 1..10 step 2
```

Iterating over this progression:

```
1  for (i in progression) {
2      println(i)
3  }
```

Results in the output:

```
1
3
5
7
9
```

To create a decreasing progression, Kotlin offers the `downTo` function. Here is how to create a progression that decreases from 5 to 1:

```
1  val downProgression: IntProgression = 5 downTo 1
```

This progression can be iterated in the same way as previous examples:

```
1  for (i in downProgression) {
2      println(i)
3  }
```

Yielding the following output:

```
5
4
3
2
1
```

It is evident that ranges and progressions in Kotlin offer concise syntax for defining and iterating over sequences of values. Understanding how to effectively use these constructs enables developers to write cleaner and more efficient Kotlin code, particularly when dealing with loops or sequences of numbers or characters.

5.11   Introduction to Kotlin's Collection APIs

Kotlin significantly simplifies collection manipulation through its rich set of APIs. Let's delve into the architecture and capabilities of Kotlin's Collection APIs, highlighting their flexibility and power.

Kotlin manages collections through its Collection interface, which is the root of the collection hierarchy. Concrete collection types, such as List, Set, and Map, extend this interface to provide specific behaviors. The primary distinction in Kotlin's collection types lies between mutable and immutable collections, each serving different purposes in application development.

- Immutable collections, which include `listOf`, `setOf`, and `mapOf`, are read-only. These are ideal for cases where a collection is not expected to change once initialized. They contribute to safer code by preventing unintended modifications.

- Mutable collections, provided by `mutableListOf`, `mutableSetOf`, and `mutableMapOf`, can be modified after initialization. These are essential for scenarios where the collection's content needs to change dynamically.

Both mutable and immutable collections share a set of common operations, which allow developers to perform essential data manipulation tasks succinctly and expressively. Operations such as filtering, mapping, and sorting are standardized, facilitating a uniform development experience across collection types.

```
1  val numbers = listOf(1, 2, 3, 4, 5)
2  val evenNumbers = numbers.filter { it % 2 == 0 }
3  val doubled = numbers.map { it * 2 }
```

In the above example, `filter` and `map` functions are applied to a list of integers. The `filter` function selects even numbers, whereas `map` function doubles each number. These operations result in the following outputs:

```
evenNumbers: [2, 4]
doubled: [2, 4, 6, 8, 10]
```

Kotlin's Collection API also emphasizes lazy evaluation through sequences (`sequenceOf`). Sequences defer the computation of collection operations until the sequence is explicitly iterated. This feature is particularly useful for handling large collections or performing complex chain operations, as it can significantly improve performance by avoiding unnecessary intermediate computations.

```
1  val numbersSequence = sequenceOf(1, 2, 3, 4, 5)
2  val filteredSequence = numbersSequence
3      .filter { it > 2 }
4      .map { it * 2 }
5      .toList() // Evaluation occurs here
```

The difference between using sequences and direct collection operations lies in the timing of evaluation. For sequences, evaluation occurs at the terminal operation (`toList`), making sequences an effective tool for optimizing performance in certain scenarios.

To facilitate working with ranges and progressions, Kotlin offers a set of functions and operators. Ranges, represented by the `..` operator, and progressions, facilitated by the downTo, step, and until functions, allow for concise expression of iterating over a sequence of numbers or characters.

```
1  for (i in 1..5) print(i) // Prints 12345
2  for (i in 5 downTo 1) print(i) // Prints 54321
3  for (i in 1..10 step 2) print(i) // Prints 13579
```

In summary, Kotlin's Collection APIs offer a flexible and powerful toolkit for managing and manipulating collections of data. By providing both mutable and immutable collections, along with a consistent set of operations and optimization tools such as sequences, Kotlin enables developers to write more expressive, efficient, and safer code.

5.12   Best Practices for Using Collections

Choosing the Correct Collection Type: The first step in using collections efficiently is to select the most appropriate type for the specific task at hand. Kotlin provides a variety of collection types, each designed for a particular set of uses.

- List is optimal for ordered collections where elements may be accessed by indices.

- Set is suitable for unique element collections, eliminating duplicates.

- Map is ideal for key-value pair collections, where each unique key maps to a specific value.

Prefer Immutability: Favor using immutable collections over mutable ones whenever possible. Immutable collections are thread-safe and less prone to errors since their content cannot be changed once initialized.

```
1  val immutableList = listOf(1, 2, 3)
```

Utilize Extension Functions: Kotlin's standard library provides a wide range of extension functions for collection types, facilitating tasks like filtering, mapping, and sorting.

```
1  val numbers = listOf(1, -2, 3, -4, 5)
2  val positives = numbers.filter { it > 0 }
3  val doubled = numbers.map { it * 2 }
```

Opt for Lazy Evaluation with Sequences: When dealing with large collections or operations that can be chained, consider using sequences to delay computation until necessary. This approach can significantly improve performance.

```
1  val sequence = sequenceOf(1, 2, 3, 4)
2  val result = sequence.map { it * 2 }
3              .filter { it > 5 }
4              .toList()
```

Minimize Memory Footprint with Views: Avoid creating unnecessary intermediate collections during chained operations. By applying asSequence, you can work with views of the original collections, reducing memory usage.

Understand the Cost of Operations: Be aware that certain collection operations, such as first, last, and indexing on linked lists, can be inefficient. Optimize your code by choosing the right collection type and operation method.

```
1  val linkedList = LinkedList(listOf(1, 2, 3))
2  val lastElement = linkedList.last // Inefficient
```

Use Collection Builders: Kotlin provides powerful APIs like buildList and buildSet for constructing collections in a more concise and expressive manner.

```
1  val customList = buildList {
2      add(1)
3      for (i in 2..5) {
4          add(i)
5      }
```

```
6   }
```

Leverage Ranges and Progressions: For creating sequences of numbers or iterating over a range, Kotlin's range expressions offer a compact and readable alternative to traditional loops.

```
1   for (i in 1..10 step 2) {
2       println(i)
3   }
```

```
1
3
5
7
9
```

Adopting these best practices when working with collections in Kotlin can vastly enhance code clarity, performance, and maintainability. Understanding and utilizing the rich set of features provided by Kotlin's collection framework allows developers to write more concise, efficient, and robust applications.

Chapter 6

Object-Oriented Programming in Kotlin

This chapter explores the object-oriented programming (OOP) features of Kotlin, which are key to building scalable and maintainable applications. It covers the core concepts of OOP, including classes, objects, inheritance, polymorphism, and encapsulation. Special attention is given to Kotlin-specific features such as data classes, object declarations, companion objects, and the seamless integration of OOP with functional programming paradigms. Through practical examples, readers will understand how Kotlin enhances traditional OOP practices with its concise syntax and innovative features, enabling the development of robust applications with less boilerplate code.

6.1 Introduction to OOP Principles in Kotlin

Object-Oriented Programming (OOP) is a paradigm that uses "objects" to design applications and computer programs. It utilizes several key concepts such as classes, objects, inheritance, polymorphism, and encapsulation, which are fundamental to creating structured and reusable code.   Kotlin, while being a modern language that incorporates functional programming concepts, also provides a robust environment for OOP. This section will discuss the integration of OOP principles in Kotlin and how it facilitates writing scalable and maintainable applications with a focus on simplicity and readability.

In Kotlin, everything is an object, which aligns with the OOP concept that aims at defining data as self-contained units (objects) with attributes and behavior (methods).   The language offers a concise and powerful syntax for declaring classes and creating objects, simplifying many aspects of traditional Java-based OOP.

- **Classes and Objects**: In Kotlin, a class is defined using the `class` keyword. It serves as a blueprint from which individual objects are created. Objects are instances of classes, containing specific values for the properties defined in the class.

- **Inheritance**: Kotlin supports inheritance, allowing a new class to inherit properties and functions from an existing class. This is accomplished using the : symbol followed by the superclass name.

- **Polymorphism**: Kotlin implements polymorphism, enabling a method to do different things based on the object that it is acting upon. Overloading and overriding are two ways Kotlin achieves polymorphism.

- **Encapsulation**: By leveraging visibility modifiers (public, private, protected, internal), Kotlin encourages encapsulation. This principle restricts direct access to some of an object's components, which is essential for safeguarding the internal state of the object and providing controlled access through methods.

Kotlin introduces several features that enhance the OOP experience:

- **Data Classes**:   Designed to hold data, these classes automatically generate `equals()`, `hashCode()`, and

146

`toString()` methods, among others, reducing boilerplate code and focusing on expressing the model's intent clearly.

- **Object Declarations**: Kotlin has a singleton pattern built into the language using the `object` keyword. This eliminates the need for traditional singletons, often verbose and error-prone in Java.

- **Companion Objects**: A Kotlin class can contain a companion object, which allows the members to be called on the class itself rather than an instance of the class, similar to static methods in Java.

Kotlin's seamless integration of OOP with functional programming paradigms provides developers with tools to create robust applications. It simplifies many complexities of OOP while retaining its benefits, making Kotlin a preferred language for many developers who seek to write concise, maintainable, and scalable applications.

Let's begin our exploration of how Kotlin implements these OOP principles in more detail, starting with defining classes and creating objects. Through practical examples, we will understand the synergy of OOP principles within the Kotlin ecosystem and how it empowers developers to architect flexible and high-quality software solutions.

6.2 Defining Classes and Creating Objects

In Kotlin, a class is a blueprint from which individual objects are created. The fundamental concept of Object-Oriented Programming (OOP) is encapsulation, and it begins with defining classes and creating instances (objects) of those classes. Kotlin's syntax for declaring classes is both concise and expressive, significantly reducing the boilerplate code commonly found in Java and other OOP languages.

Defining a Simple Class

To define a class in Kotlin, the `class` keyword is used, followed by the class name and a pair of curly braces. Here is an example of a minimal class definition:

```
class Person {
}
```

This `Person` class, as defined, is the simplest form of a class in Kotlin. It does not include any properties or methods.

Creating an Object

Objects are instances of a class. Once a class is defined, you can create objects of that class using the class name as a constructor. For instance, to create an object of the `Person` class, you would write:

```
val person = Person()
```

This statement creates an instance of `Person` and assigns it to the variable `person`.

Adding Properties to a Class

Properties are the characteristics of a class. In Kotlin, properties are declared inside the class body, and Kotlin synthesizes getters and setters for these properties, reducing the amount of code you need to write. For example:

```
class Person {
    var name: String = ""
    var age: Int = 0
}
```

This version of the `Person` class has two properties: `name` and `age`. Kotlin provides a default getter and setter for these properties. However, Kotlin also allows you to define custom accessors (getters and setters) if you need more control over how properties are accessed or modified.

Primary Constructor

Kotlin classes can have a primary constructor, which is part of the class header. It is declared following the class name:

```
1  class Person(var name: String, var age: Int) {
2  }
```

Here, the primary constructor has two parameters, name and age, which are also class properties. This concise syntax allows for the initialization of the properties directly from the constructor. When creating an instance of such a class, you must pass the required parameters:

```
1  val person = Person("John Doe", 30)
```

This statement creates a Person object with the name "John Doe" and age of 30.

Initialization Block

For more complex initialization logic that cannot be handled in the primary constructor, Kotlin provides an initialization block, which is prefixed with the init keyword:

```
1  class Person(var name: String, var age: Int) {
2      init {
3          println("Person created: \$name, \$age years old")
4      }
5  }
```

The initialization block is executed every time an instance of the class is created, allowing for additional initialization steps beyond what is done in the primary constructor.

In summary, defining classes and creating objects in Kotlin is straightforward, thanks to its concise syntax. With features like properties, primary constructors, and initialization blocks, Kotlin enhances the capabilities of traditional OOP, allowing for more expressive and efficient code.

6.3   Constructor and Initialization Blocks

In Kotlin, the concept of constructors is a cornerstone in the creation of instances of a class. A constructor is a special member function of a class that is called when an object of the class is created. It essentially initializes new objects. Kotlin offers a primary constructor and one or more secondary constructors to enable this initialization process.

Primary Constructor

The primary constructor is part of the class header. It is concise and designed to handle most straightforward initialization scenarios. The syntax for declaring a primary constructor is as follows:

```
1  class ClassName constructor(parameter1: Type1, parameter2: Type2) {
2      // class body
3  }
```

The keyword `constructor` is optional if the primary constructor has no annotations or visibility modifiers. Parameters defined in the primary constructor can be used for initializing properties directly. The following is an example of a class with a primary constructor and property initialization:

```
1  class Person(val name: String, var age: Int)
```

In this case, `Person` class has a primary constructor with two parameters, `name` and `age`. The properties are directly initialized with these parameters.

Initialization Blocks

For more complex initialization logic that cannot be handled in the primary constructor, Kotlin provides initializer blocks. These blocks are prefixed with the init keyword and can access the parameters of the primary constructor. If a class has multiple initializer blocks, they are executed sequentially in the order they appear in the class body. An example of using an initializer block is given below:

```
class Person(val name: String, var age: Int) {
    init {
        require(age > 0) { "Age must be positive" }
    }
}
```

In this example, the init block contains a check to ensure that the age parameter is positive. If age is not greater than 0, an IllegalArgumentException is thrown.

Secondary Constructors

Kotlin also allows for secondary constructors. These are useful when a class needs to provide multiple ways of initialization. Each secondary constructor must delegate to the primary constructor, directly or indirectly, allowing for a unified initialization process across all constructors. To declare a secondary constructor, use the constructor keyword inside the class body:

```
class Person(val name: String, var age: Int) {
    constructor(name: String, age: Int, city: String) : this(name, age)
        {
        // additional processing
    }
}
```

In this example, the Person class has a secondary constructor that accepts an additional parameter, city. It delegates to the primary constructor using the this keyword before performing any additional initialization.

Understanding constructors and initialization blocks in Kotlin is vital for performing object initialization and ensuring instances are properly constructed before use. The flexibility of these components allows developers to implement concise, safe, and readable initialization logic in their classes.

6.4   Properties and Fields: Getters and Setters

Properties and fields constitute the backbone of data encapsulation in Kotlin, a principle that is central to the object-oriented programming paradigm. Properties in Kotlin serve as a gateway for accessing the fields of a class, thus allowing for controlled interaction with the object's state. Unlike many other programming languages, Kotlin simplifies the implementation of getters and setters through its property mechanism.

When a property is defined in a Kotlin class, the compiler automatically generates a field (backing field), a getter, and a setter (for var properties) under the hood. This feature significantly reduces the boilerplate code associated with property access mechanisms in languages like Java.

Defining Properties

Properties in Kotlin are defined using the keywords val (for read-only properties) and var (for mutable properties). Here is a basic example:

```
1  class Person {
2      var name: String = "John Doe"
3      val age: Int = 30
4  }
```

In this example, name is a mutable property, whereas age is read-only. The Kotlin compiler automatically provides a default getter for age and both a getter and setter for name.

Custom Getters and Setters

Kotlin allows the customization of getters and setters, offering greater control over how property values are accessed and modified. This is particularly useful for implementing validation, logging, or other side effects when properties are accessed or modified.

For instance, to enforce a non-negative age for a Person class, a custom setter can be used:

```
class Person(var name: String, initialAge: Int) {
    var age: Int = initialAge
        set(value) {
            if (value >= 0) field = value
            else throw IllegalArgumentException("Age cannot be negative"
            )
        }
}
```

In the custom setter for age, field refers to the backing field of age. The custom setter logic checks if the new value is non-negative before assigning it to field; otherwise, it throws an IllegalArgumentException.

Visibility of Getters and Setters

Kotlin enables the customization of the visibility of getters and setters independently from the property they belong to. This allows, for instance, a property to be publicly readable but more restrictively mutable.

To illustrate, making the setter of name private in the Person class:

```
class Person {
    var name: String = "John Doe"
        private set
}
```

This code snippet ensures that name can be modified only within the Person class, despite being readable from any context where a Person instance is accessible.

153

Properties and their accompanying getters and setters play a crucial role in Kotlin's simplification of object-oriented programming. By automatically generating the necessary boilerplate associated with field access and modification, and by providing flexibility through custom getters and setters, Kotlin offers a significantly improved developer experience.

6.5   Inheritance in Kotlin: Overriding Methods and Properties

Inheritance is a fundamental concept in object-oriented programming that allows a class to inherit properties and methods from another class. Kotlin, with its support for modern programming practices, provides a comprehensive approach to inheritance, ensuring code reusability and extending the functionality of existing codes. This section elucidates the mechanism of inheritance in Kotlin, focusing on overriding methods and properties, and the syntax that facilitates these operations.

To begin with, let's define a base class in Kotlin. In Kotlin, all classes are by default final; hence, they cannot be inherited. To allow a class to be inherited, it must be marked with the open keyword.

```
1  open class Animal {
2      open fun speak() {
3          println("This animal makes a sound.")
4      }
5  }
```

In the above example, the Animal class contains an open method speak, which allows it to be overridden in derived classes. The open modifier is essential because, by default, methods are final in Kotlin.

To inherit from the Animal class, the syntax is straightforward. The derived class uses the : symbol followed by the superclass name. Below is an example of a Dog class inheriting from Animal.

```
1  class Dog : Animal() {
```

```
2    override fun speak() {
3        println("The dog barks.")
4    }
5  }
```

When the `Dog` class overrides the `speak` method, it must use the `override` modifier. This explicitly states that the method is an overridden version of its superclass method. Overriding is a mechanism that allows a subclass to provide a specific implementation of a method that is already defined in its superclass.

Additionally, Kotlin supports the overriding of properties. Similar to methods, properties in the superclass must be marked with the `open` modifier, and the subclass must use the `override` modifier. Consider the following example where a property is overridden.

```
1  open class Bird {
2      open val color: String = "Grey"
3  }
4
5  class Parrot : Bird() {
6      override val color: String = "Green"
7  }
```

In this example, the `Bird` class has an open property `color` which is overridden by the `Parrot` class. The overriding mechanism for properties works in the same way as it does for methods, allowing subclasses to provide specific values or behaviours.

Understanding the concept of inheritance and the ability to override methods and properties is crucial for Kotlin developers. It enables the extension and customization of existing classes, promoting code reusability and maintainability. Kotlin's straightforward syntax for inheritance and overriding makes it a powerful feature for developing scalable and robust applications.

To summarize inheritance and method overriding in Kotlin:

- Use the `open` modifier to allow a class or member to be inherited or overridden.

- Employ the `override` modifier in the subclass to override a method or property of its superclass.

- Overridden methods and properties allow subclasses to provide specific implementations, enhancing the flexibility and functionality of object-oriented Kotlin programs.

By mastering inheritance and overriding in Kotlin, developers can effectively leverage the principles of object-oriented programming to build sophisticated and adaptable software systems.

6.6 Abstract Classes and Interfaces

Kotlin provides powerful concepts to design and architect software through abstract classes and interfaces. These concepts aid in creating a blueprint for classes to follow, ensuring a standardized approach to solving problems within a software application.

Abstract Classes

An abstract class is a class that cannot be instantiated directly. To use an abstract class, a subclass must inherit from the abstract class and provide implementations for the abstract members. Abstract classes are declared using the `abstract` keyword. An abstract class may contain both abstract and non-abstract members. Abstract members do not have an implementation in the abstract class, thus they must be overridden by the subclass.

Here is an example of defining an abstract class and inheriting from it:

```
abstract class Vehicle {
    abstract fun accelerate()
    fun stop() {
        println("The vehicle has stopped.")
    }
}


class Car : Vehicle() {
    override fun accelerate() {
```

```
10          println("The car is accelerating.")
11       }
12  }
```

In this example, the `Vehicle` class is abstract and has an abstract method named *accelerate*. The `Car` class inherits from `Vehicle` and provides an implementation for the *accelerate* method. Thus, the `Car` class can be instantiated, but the `Vehicle` class cannot.

Interfaces

Interfaces in Kotlin are similar to abstract classes but are more flexible and lightweight. An interface defines a contract for classes to implement. interfaces can contain abstract methods as well as method implementations. However, interfaces cannot contain any state.

An interface can be defined using the `interface` keyword. Here is an example:

```
1   interface Drivable {
2       fun accelerate()
3       fun brake() {
4           println("The vehicle is braking.")
5       }
6   }
7
8   class Bicycle : Drivable {
9       override fun accelerate() {
10          println("The bicycle is accelerating.")
11      }
12      // No need to override `brake` as it already has a default
            implementation.
13  }
```

In this example, the `Drivable` interface contains an abstract method *accelerate* and a default method *brake*. The `Bicycle` class implements the `Drivable` interface and provides its own implementation of *accelerate*. Since *brake* has a default implementation in the `Drivable` interface, it is not mandatory for the `Bicycle` class to override it, but it can choose to do so.

157

Choosing Between Abstract Classes and Interfaces

Deciding whether to use an abstract class or an interface depends on the design requirements of the application. Use abstract classes when you want to share a common base implementation among multiple related classes. Interfaces are more suited to providing a common functionality that can be adopted by unrelated classes. With Kotlin's support for implementing multiple interfaces, they offer more flexibility compared to abstract classes. However, Kotlin's use of default implementations in interfaces blurs the lines, allowing interfaces to somewhat mimic abstract classes.

Remember, abstract classes and interfaces are not mutually exclusive; they can be used together to create a robust and flexible design.

6.7   Visibility Modifiers: Public, Private, Protected, and Internal

Visibility modifiers in Kotlin control where a class, interface, function, or property can be accessed from. These are essential for encapsulation, one of the core principles of object-oriented programming. Kotlin provides four visibility modifiers: `public`, `private`, `protected`, and `internal`. The default visibility is `public` if no modifier is specified.

Public Modifier

The `public` modifier allows the entity it is attached to be accessible from any other part of the program or module. Since it's the default modifier, entities without a declared visibility modifier are public. This is useful for classes, interfaces, functions, and properties meant to be accessed globally across modules.

```
1  public class PublicExample {
2      public val exampleProperty = "Accessible anywhere"
3
4      public fun exampleFunction() {
```

```
5        println("This function can be called from anywhere.")
6    }
7 }
```

Private Modifier

The `private` modifier restricts access to the entity within the scope it
was defined. For a class or interface member, this means it can only
be accessed within the containing class or interface. For top-level
declarations, access is restricted to within the same file.

```
1  class PrivateExample {
2      private val exampleProperty = "Accessible only within this class"
3
4      private fun exampleFunction() {
5          println("This function can only be called inside this class.")
6      }
7  }
8
9  fun main() {
10     val example = PrivateExample()
11     // example.exampleFunction() // Error: Cannot access '
          exampleFunction': it is private in 'PrivateExample'
12 }
```

Protected Modifier

The `protected` modifier is similar to `private`, with the addition that
it also allows access from subclasses. It cannot be used for top-level
declarations.

```
1  open class BaseClass {
2      protected val exampleProperty = "Accessible within this class and
          subclasses"
3  }
4
5  class DerivedClass : BaseClass() {
6      fun printProperty() {
7          println(exampleProperty) // Accessible due to being protected
8      }
9  }
```

Internal Modifier

The `internal` modifier allows access to the entity within the same module. A module in Kotlin is a set of Kotlin files compiled together. It could be an IntelliJ IDEA module, a Maven or Gradle project, or a set of files compiled with the same invocation of the Kotlin compiler.

```
1  internal class InternalExample {
2      internal val exampleProperty = "Accessible within the same module"
3
4      internal fun exampleFunction() {
5          println("This function can be accessed within the same module.")
6      }
7  }
```

By carefully selecting the appropriate visibility modifier, you can design your Kotlin programs with encapsulation in mind. This not only improves program structure and readability but also ensures that internal implementation details are not exposed where they should not be.

6.8   Data Classes and Destructuring Declarations

Data classes in Kotlin are a powerful feature designed to hold data in a concise manner. Unlike regular classes, which typically encapsulate behavior and data, data classes are primarily used to store state. They are declared using the `data` keyword preceding the `class` keyword. This informs the compiler that the class is intended to act as a data holder, resulting in the automatic generation of several utility functions such as `equals()`, `hashCode()`, and `toString()`, which are essential for comparing and printing the contents of the class in a standardized format.

```
1  data class User(val name: String, val age: Int)
```

The example above demonstrates a simple data class definition with two properties: name and age. It's worth noting that the primary constructor needs to have at least one parameter. These parameters are automatically converted to member properties, thereby reducing the boilerplate code needed to define simple classes to hold data.

Another distinctive feature of data classes is their capability to support destructuring declarations. This functionality allows you to easily decompose a data class object into a number of variables, each corresponding to a property of the class.

```kotlin
val jane = User("Jane Doe", 30)
val (name, age) = jane
println("Name: $name, Age: $age")
```

In the code snippet above, the jane object is destructured into two variables, name and age, which are then used within a print statement. This feature significantly improves the readability and conciseness of data handling in Kotlin.

Data classes also facilitate the copy operation with the copy() function. This function, generated automatically by the Kotlin compiler, allows for the creation of a new instance of a data class, copying the properties of an existing instance with the option to modify some of the properties.

```kotlin
val john = jane.copy(name = "John Doe")
```

In this example, a new User instance, john, is created from jane with the name property changed to "John Doe". This exemplifies the ease with which data models can be manipulated while maintaining immutability, an important aspect of functional programming paradigms that Kotlin supports.

Furthermore, this section would not be complete without mentioning the inherent compatibility of data classes with Kotlin's functional features such as high-order functions and collection processing functions. For instance, consider the scenario where we have a list of User objects and we wish to filter and transform this collection:

```kotlin
val users = listOf(User("Alice", 28), User("Bob", 31), User("Charlie",
    25))
val namesOfUsersAbove30 = users.filter { it.age > 30 }.map { it.name }
```

161

```
3   println(namesOfUsersAbove30)
```

```
[Bob]
```

In this example, the `filter` and `map` functions are used in conjunction to identify users older than 30 years and then transform the filtered list into a list of their names. This showcases how data classes, together with Kotlin's collection processing capabilities, facilitate concise and expressive data manipulation.

In summary, data classes and destructuring declarations enhance Kotlin's offering as a modern language that reduces verbosity whilst improving the readability and maintainability of code. These features underscore Kotlin's capacity to succinctly handle data, a crucial aspect of developing maintainable and scalable applications.

6.9   Object Expressions and Declarations: Anonymous and Companion Objects

Kotlin provides a unique facility to quickly instantiate an object of an anonymous class that inherits from another class or implements an interface, known as object expressions. Furthermore, the language introduces the concept of companion objects, which serves as an elegant solution to the absence of static members, commonly found in other programming languages.

Object Expressions

Object expressions are primarily used when one requires a slight modification of some class or interface without declaring a new subclass for it. The syntax of an object expression is straightforward: it is prefixed by the `object` keyword followed by a colon (:) and the class or interface to modify.

Consider an example where one needs an `OnClickListener` for a button in an Android application, which can be succinctly implemented using an object expression:

```
button.setOnClickListener(object : View.OnClickListener {
    override fun onClick(v: View?) {
        // Handle the button click
    }
})
```

The key aspect of object expressions is that they enable you to declare and instantiate an anonymous class in one go, making the code concise and readable.

Companion Objects

In Kotlin, static members are replaced with companion objects, allowing you to attach functions and properties to a class rather than its instances. A companion object is declared within a class with the `companion` keyword, and its members can be accessed using the class name as a qualifier, not unlike static members in Java or C++.

The companion object is useful for factory methods, constants, and utility functions that should be tied to a class rather than any instance of it. Here is an example showing how to define and use a companion object:

```
class MyClass {
    companion object Factory {
        fun create(): MyClass = MyClass()
    }
}
```

To create a new instance of `MyClass` using the companion object's factory method:

```
val instance = MyClass.create()
```

It's important to note that, despite their typical use, companion objects are not exactly synonymous with static methods in other languages. They are, in fact, object instances themselves, bound to a class type rather than class instances. This distinction allows companion objects to implement interfaces and hold state if required, offering a more flexible design paradigm than static members.

In summary, object expressions and declarations in Kotlin, particularly anonymous and companion objects, provide powerful tools to developers for creating concise, flexible, and maintainable code. Through the use of these constructs, Kotlin addresses common design and implementation patterns in a way that is both innovative and in harmony with the language's overall philosophy of pragmatism and conciseness.

6.10   Extension   Functions/Properties   for Classes

Extension functions and properties provide a powerful mechanism in Kotlin for adding new functionalities to classes without inheriting from them. This capability is particularly useful when working with classes from a library to which you do not have the source code or cannot modify directly for other reasons. Essentially, extension functions and properties allow for the adherent principles of encapsulation to be maintained while still offering the flexibility to augment the capabilities of a class.

To declare an extension function, one must prefix the name of the class to be extended to the function name, separated by a dot. This makes the first parameter of the function the instance of the object on which the function is called, accessible within the function body through the 'this' keyword. The general syntax for defining an extension function is as follows:

```
1  fun ClassName.extensionFunctionName(params): ReturnType {
2      // function body
3  }
```

Consider extending the 'String' class with a function to count the number of vowels it contains:

```
1  fun String.countVowels(): Int {
2      var count = 0
3      for (char in this) {
4          if (char in "aeiouAEIOU") {
5              count++
6          }
7      }
8      return count
9  }
```

After defining this extension function, it can be used on any 'String' object as if it were a member function of the 'String' class:

```
val vowelCount = "hello world".countVowels()  // Returns 3
```

Extension properties can similarly be used to add new properties to a class. Unlike functions, extension properties cannot hold a state and therefore must be defined using either a getter or a setter, but not both. The syntax for defining an extension property is as follows:

```
1  val ClassName.extensionPropertyName: PropertyType
2      get() = // property getter logic
```

For instance, adding a 'isPalindrome' extension property to the 'String' class can be done as follows:

```
1  val String.isPalindrome: Boolean
2      get() = this == this.reversed()
```

This property can then be accessed like any other property of the 'String' class:

```
val palindromeCheck = "madam".isPalindrome  // Returns true
```

It is crucial to understand that extension functions and properties do not actually modify the classes they extend. Instead, they provide a syntactic sugar for calling static functions in a way that appears as though new functionality has been added to the class. This implies that extensions are resolved statically at compile-time rather than dynamically at runtime, and the actual type of the

165

variable determines which extension function or property is called, not the type determined through polymorphism at runtime.

In summary, extension functions and properties are a versatile feature in Kotlin, offering an elegant solution for augmenting classes with new functionalities in a way that respects the principles of encapsulation and adheres to the type safety that Kotlin enforces.

6.11   Sealed Classes and Enum Classes

Sealed classes and enum classes in Kotlin extend the language's capabilities for handling a limited set of types more elegantly. This section focuses on both constructs, outlining their purposes, usage, and the benefits they offer in the context of Kotlin's type system.

Sealed Classes

Sealed classes are used to represent restricted class hierarchies, where a value can have one of the types from a limited set, but cannot have any other type. This feature ensures when you use a sealed class, you can handle all possible cases explicitly, making your code more safe and predictable.

In Kotlin, sealed classes are declared with the `sealed` modifier:

```
1  sealed class ApiResponse
```

What distinguishes sealed classes from regular classes is the ability to have subclasses, but only within the same file. This makes the sealed classes more controlled. For example, you might want to define a limited set of responses from a network operation:

```
1  sealed class ApiResponse {
2      data class Success(val data: String) : ApiResponse()
3      data class Error(val error: Throwable) : ApiResponse()
4      object Loading : ApiResponse()
5  }
```

The benefit of using sealed classes comes into play when using when expression for exhaustive checking without needing an else clause.

```
1  fun handleResponse(response: ApiResponse) = when(response) {
2      is ApiResponse.Success -> println("Data: ${response.data}")
3      is ApiResponse.Error -> println("Error: ${response.error}")
4      is ApiResponse.Loading -> println("Loading...")
5  }
```

Because all the possible subclasses of `ApiResponse` are known, the compiler can guarantee that all cases are covered in the when expression, enhancing safety.

Enum Classes

Enum classes in Kotlin are another way to model types that represent a fixed set of constants. Like in Java, Kotlin enums are much more powerful than enums in languages like C++. They can have properties, methods, and even implement interfaces.

Defining an enum class is straightforward:

```
1  enum class Direction {
2      NORTH, SOUTH, EAST, WEST
3  }
```

Enum constants can also have associated values:

```
1  enum class HttpStatusCode(val code: Int) {
2      OK(200),
3      NOT_FOUND(404),
4      INTERNAL_SERVER_ERROR(500);
5  }
```

And you can access these properties like you would with any other object:

```
1  println(HttpStatusCode.OK.code) // Output: 200
```

Furthermore, enum classes in Kotlin can declare methods:

```
1  enum class HttpStatusCode(val code: Int) {
2      OK(200),
```

```
3    NOT_FOUND(404),
4    INTERNAL_SERVER_ERROR(500);
5
6    fun description(): String = when(this) {
7        OK -> "Request succeeded."
8        NOT_FOUND -> "The requested resource was not found."
9        INTERNAL_SERVER_ERROR -> "The server encountered an error."
10   }
11 }
```

Enum classes bring structure and a higher level of abstraction to Kotlin's type system, making handling a fixed set of constants more straightforward and semantically rich.

Choosing Between Sealed and Enum Classes

The choice between sealed and enum classes depends on the use case. Use enum classes when you have an enumeration of well-known values and their number does not tend to change. On the other hand, sealed classes are preferable when dealing with a class hierarchy representing a closed set of types which might be extended within the same module, allowing for more complex object-oriented design patterns.

Both sealed and enum classes play a significant role in writing expressive and type-safe Kotlin code, leveraging the language's features for better compile-time checks and reducing runtime errors.

6.12   Delegation: By Lazy and By Delegated Properties

Delegation is a powerful feature in Kotlin programming, enabling more concise and maintainable code by allowing certain responsibilities to be delegated to another property or class. Specifically, Kotlin offers two noteworthy delegation patterns: by lazy and by delegated properties. These patterns enhance the capability to defer the initialization of variables and to customize the behavior of properties, respectively.

By Lazy

The lazy delegation is particularly useful when dealing with expensive operations that should only be executed when needed. Essentially, it postpones the initialization of a value until the first time it is accessed. This is beneficial for resources that may not be used immediately or at all during the execution of a program. The lazy function is thread-safe by default, ensuring that the value is only calculated once even in a multithreaded environment, but other initialization modes can be chosen to optimize performance based on the application's requirements.

An example usage of lazy is shown below:

```
val heavyResource: Resource by lazy {
    println("Initializing heavy resource...")
    Resource()
}
```

In the above example, the Resource instance is not created at the point of the variable declaration but at the moment heavyResource is first accessed. This defers the loading time and memory usage of initiating Resource until it is actually needed.

By Delegated Properties

Kotlin also supports a broader delegation model through delegated properties, allowing the behavior of properties (such as getters and setters) to be delegated to another class. This is achieved using the by keyword followed by an instance of a class that provides the necessary logic for the property operations.

A common use case for this is observing changes to a property, also known as property delegation. Kotlin provides a utility class Delegates.observable() for this:

```
import kotlin.properties.Delegates

var observedValue: Int by Delegates.observable(0) { property, oldValue,
    newValue ->
    println("$property changed from $oldValue to $newValue")
```

169

```
5  }
```

When `observedValue` is modified, the lambda expression passed to the `observable()` method is invoked, allowing the change to be recorded, validated, or even vetoed.

Both delegation patterns—by lazy and by delegated properties—illustrate Kotlin's flexibility and the elegance with which it supports advanced programming paradigms. These features converge to enhance the language's simplicity, robustness, and performance, making Kotlin a preferred choice for modern software development projects.

Custom Delegated Properties

For scenarios beyond what the standard library offers, Kotlin allows for the creation of custom delegated properties. To define a custom delegate, a class needs to implement the operator methods `getValue()` and `setValue()` for mutable properties.

Here's a simple custom delegate example:

```
1   import kotlin.reflect.KProperty
2
3   class ExampleDelegate {
4       private var backingField = "Default"
5
6       operator fun getValue(thisRef: Any?, property: KProperty<*>):
            String {
7           println("${property.name} returns $backingField")
8           return backingField
9       }
10
11      operator fun setValue(thisRef: Any?, property: KProperty<*>, value:
            String) {
12          println("${property.name} changes from $backingField to $value")
13          backingField = value
14      }
15  }
16
17  var exampleProperty: String by ExampleDelegate()
```

This flexibility opens a realm of possibilities, allowing developers to encapsulate complex property behavior within reusable delegate classes, thus promoting clean and DRY (Don't Repeat Yourself) code.

To summarize, Kotlin's support for delegation via the `lazy` function and delegated properties streamlines the development of efficient and effective Kotlin applications. By harnessing these features, developers can write less boilerplate, more readable, and more expressive code.

Chapter 7

Exploring Kotlin Coroutines for Asynchronous Programming

The chapter on exploring Kotlin coroutines introduces the powerful concurrency model built into the Kotlin language, designed to simplify the development of asynchronous and non-blocking code. Coroutines provide a way to write complex asynchronous code that is both easy to understand and efficient. The chapter covers the basics of coroutines, including their setup, the use of various builders like launch and async, and how to manage contexts and scopes effectively. It also delves into more advanced topics such as error handling, flow control, and combining coroutines for complex operations. By learning to effectively leverage coroutines, readers will be able to improve the responsiveness and performance of their Kotlin applications.

7.1 Introduction to Asynchronous Programming

Asynchronous programming is a paradigm that allows for non-linear execution of tasks. Unlike synchronous programming, where tasks are executed in a sequence, one after the other, asynchronous programming does not block the execution thread while waiting for a task to complete. This approach is especially beneficial in environments where tasks are I/O bound or network bound, such as in web servers or applications with graphical user interface (GUI).

One of the key concepts in asynchronous programming is the event loop. The event loop is a programming construct that waits for and dispatches events or messages in a program. It works by repeatedly collecting events from an event queue and dispatching them to the appropriate handlers for processing. This mechanism allows a single program thread to manage multiple concurrent operations.

To illustrate the difference between synchronous and asynchronous execution, consider the following example in a hypothetical programming language:

```
1   # Synchronous code
2   print("Start")
3   result = performLongOperation()
4   print("Result: " + result)
5   print("End")
6
7   # Asynchronous code
8   print("Start")
9   performLongOperationAsync(callback: (result) => {
10      print("Result: " + result)
11  })
12  print("End")
```

In the synchronous code example, the print statement "End" would not execute until `performLongOperation` completes, potentially causing a significant delay if the operation is time-consuming. In contrast, in the asynchronous code example, the print statement "End" is executed immediately after the long operation is initiated.

The result of the long operation is handled separately by a callback function, allowing the main program to continue running without waiting.

Asynchronous programming in Kotlin is facilitated by coroutines, which are lightweight threads. Coroutines are managed by the Kotlin runtime rather than the operating system, allowing for efficient execution of thousands of concurrent tasks. This model provides a more straightforward way to handle asynchronous operations compared to traditional methods such as callbacks or futures and promises found in other languages.

To effectively use asynchronous programming, especially with Kotlin coroutines, developers need to understand the concepts of *suspending functions*, *coroutine builders*, and *coroutine scopes*. Suspending functions are at the heart of Kotlin's asynchronous model, enabling the suspension of a coroutine's execution without blocking the underlying thread. Coroutine builders, such as `launch` and `async`, are used to start coroutines within specified scopes, controlling their lifecycle and execution context.

This section sets the foundation for understanding how asynchrony works and prepares the reader for more detailed discussions on Kotlin's coroutine-based approach to asynchronous programming in the following sections.

7.2 Understanding Coroutines in Kotlin

Coroutines in Kotlin embody a powerful programming model that fosters writing asynchronous, non-blocking code. Conceptually, coroutines are lightweight threads. However, unlike threads, they do not operate on their separate stacks. This characteristic drastically reduces the overhead associated with context switching and resource consumption, making coroutines a more scalable option for concurrency.

To comprehend the fundamentals of coroutines, it is essential to understand their two main components: the coroutine builders and the suspension points.

Coroutine Builders

In Kotlin, coroutines are initiated using builders. The most
commonly used coroutine builders are launch and async. These
builders establish a block of code that executes within a coroutine.

```
1  import kotlinx.coroutines.*
2
3  fun main() {
4      GlobalScope.launch {
5          // Code to run in coroutine
6      }
7  }
```

The GlobalScope.launch function starts a new coroutine that runs
in the background. The 'GlobalScope' implies that the lifecycle of the
coroutine is bound to the application's lifecycle.

Another significant builder is async, which is used for computations
that result in a value. The async builder returns a Deferred type,
which is a non-blocking future that represents a promise to provide
a result later.

```
1   import kotlinx.coroutines.*
2
3   fun main() = runBlocking {
4       val deferred: Deferred<Int> = async {
5           // Code that computes a result
6           42
7       }
8
9       println("Computed: ${deferred.await()}")
10  }
```

In the example above, the await() function is called to retrieve the result of the async computation, suspending the coroutine if the value
is not yet available, without blocking the thread.

Suspension Points

Suspension points are at the heart of coroutines, enabling the suspension of the execution of a coroutine, freeing the thread for other tasks without disrupting the flow of the coroutine's logic. A function is marked as suspend to indicate that it can suspend the execution of a coroutine.

```
1  suspend fun fetchDoc(id: String): Document {
2      // Fetch document from network or database, can suspend
3  }
```

The suspend keyword does not imply that a function will always suspend execution, but it allows the function to do so. This mechanism is critical for operations that involve waiting, such as network requests or database operations, enabling the efficient use of system resources.

Coroutine Context and Dispatchers

Every coroutine has a context, represented by the CoroutineContext interface, which encapsulates various elements of the coroutine's environment, including its dispatcher. Dispatchers determine the thread or thread pool on which the coroutine will execute. Kotlin provides multiple dispatchers, like Dispatchers.Default for CPU-intensive workloads and Dispatchers.IO for I/O operations.

```
1  GlobalScope.launch(Dispatchers.IO) {
2      // Coroutine that performs I/O operations
3  }
```

It is critical to match the nature of the coroutine's work to an appropriate dispatcher to maximize performance and resource efficiency.

By understanding these key aspects of coroutines in Kotlin, developers can harness their full potential to write concise, expressive, and efficient asynchronous code.

7.3   Setting up the Coroutine Environment

To begin integrating coroutines into a Kotlin project, it is essential to
first establish the appropriate environment. This involves including
the necessary dependencies in your project and understanding how
to configure the Kotlin compiler for coroutines. This section provides
a comprehensive guide to setting up the coroutine environment in
your Kotlin project.

First and foremost, you need to add the coroutine library
dependency to your project. Kotlin coroutines are not included in
the standard library, hence the need for explicit inclusion. If you are
using Gradle as your build system, include the following lines in
your build.gradle file:

```
1  dependencies {
2      implementation "org.jetbrains.kotlinx:kotlinx-coroutines-core:1.5.0
       "
3  }
```

Make sure to check for the latest version of the coroutines library to
ensure compatibility and access to the latest features. Including this
dependency provides you with the basic coroutine builders and functions required to start writing asynchronous code using coroutines in
Kotlin.

Next, configure your Kotlin compiler to enable coroutine support.
This step is crucial for the Kotlin compiler to understand the
coroutine-specific syntax and semantics. In your build.gradle file,
add the following compiler argument under the Kotlin compilation
tasks:

```
1  kotlin {
2      sourceSets {
3          main.kotlin.srcDirs += 'src/main/kotlin'
4      }
5      tasks.withType(org.jetbrains.kotlin.gradle.tasks.KotlinCompile).all
           {
6          kotlinOptions {
7              freeCompilerArgs += "-Xopt-in=kotlinx.coroutines.
                   ExperimentalCoroutinesApi"
8          }
```

```
9        }
10   }
```

The   compiler   argument
-Xopt-in=kotlinx.coroutines.ExperimentalCoroutinesApi
signals the Kotlin compiler that your project is opting into the
experimental features provided by the coroutines library. It is
worth noting that certain features in the coroutines library are
marked as experimental and might change in future versions. By
opting in, you acknowledge the use of these features while being
aware of their experimental nature.

After setting up the dependencies and compiler configuration, verify
your setup by writing a simple coroutine using the launch builder in
a Kotlin application:

```
1    import kotlinx.coroutines.*
2
3    fun main() {
4        GlobalScope.launch {
5            delay(1000L)
6            println("World!")
7        }
8        println("Hello,")
9        Thread.sleep(2000L)
10   }
```

Executing the above code snippet should produce the following output:

```
Hello,
World!
```

This simple example demonstrates a coroutine launched in the
GlobalScope, which after a delay of 1000 milliseconds, prints
"World!" to the console. The Thread.sleep(2000L) call in the main
thread ensures that the JVM stays alive long enough for the
coroutine to execute.

By following the steps outlined in this section, you have successfully
set up the coroutine environment in your Kotlin project. This setup
enables you to begin utilizing coroutines for asynchronous program-

ming, significantly improving the responsiveness and performance of your Kotlin applications.

7.4 Basic Coroutine Builders: launch and async

Coroutines in Kotlin are foundational to achieving asynchronous programming. Among the building blocks offered, two primary coroutine builders stand out for their versatility and ease of use: launch and async. Understanding the capabilities and ideal use cases for each of these builders enables developers to harness the full potential of coroutines in their applications.

The launch builder is used to start a new coroutine that does not have any result as an outcome. Instead, its purpose is to execute a piece of code that operates asynchronously. The launch builder is typically used for tasks where the outcome of the coroutine is not directly needed. When a coroutine is launched using launch, it returns a Job object, which can be used to manage the execution of the coroutine, for example, cancellation.

```
1   import kotlinx.coroutines.*
2
3   fun main() = runBlocking {
4       val job = launch { // launch a new coroutine
5           delay(1000L) // non-blocking delay for 1 second
6           println("World!") // print after delay
7       }
8       print("Hello, ") // main coroutine continues while the launched one
            is delayed
9       job.join() // wait until the launched coroutine completes
10  }
```

The async builder, on the other hand, is used for coroutines that compute a value and return it. The key distinction is that async returns an instance of Deferred<T>, which represents a promise of a future value. Deferred is a subtype of Job, with the added functionality that it can yield a result through its await() method. This makes async ideal for when the result of an asynchronous computation is needed.

```
1   import kotlinx.coroutines.*
2
3   fun main() = runBlocking {
4       val deferred: Deferred<Int> = async { // async returns a Deferred
            value
5           delay(1000L) // simulate long-running computation
6           42 // return value after delay
7       }
8       println("The answer is ${deferred.await()}") // use await to get
            the result
9   }
```

An important concept to grasp is structured concurrency, which both launch and async adhere to when used inside a coroutine scope. Structured concurrency ensures that coroutines are executed within defined scopes, thereby preventing leaks and unwarranted running coroutines.

Understanding the difference between launch and async is vital for applying the correct builder in various situations. Launch is best suited for fire-and-forget scenarios, where executing a block of code asynchronously is required, but its result is not directly needed. Conversely, async should be employed when the outcome of the coroutine is of interest, as it allows for the result to be awaited and utilized upon completion.

Additionally, it's important to note that both builders can take a CoroutineContext parameter, allowing for fine-grained control over coroutine execution, such as specifying the dispatcher for thread management.

- Use launch for tasks where you do not need to compute a result.

- Use async when you need to compute a result asynchronously and use it later.

- Both builders enforce structured concurrency, promoting safer and more predictable coroutine management.

- The choice of the builder affects how you manage and retrieve the outcome of your asynchronous operations.

In summary, selecting the appropriate coroutine builder and understanding its usage are critical in leveraging Kotlin's coroutine-based asynchronous programming capabilities effectively.

7.5 Structured Concurrency and Coroutine Scope

Structured concurrency is a programming paradigm within Kotlin coroutines designed to improve the manageability and safety of concurrent execution. The concept revolves around the orderly execution, completion, and cleanup of concurrent operations, ensuring that the lifecycles of asynchronous tasks are properly confined within a defined structure, thus preventing common concurrency issues such as leaks and unintended execution.

In the context of Kotlin coroutines, structured concurrency is implemented through coroutine scopes. A coroutine scope controls the lifecycle of coroutines, ensuring that all launched coroutines complete their execution before the scope itself completes. This means that a parent coroutine will not complete until all its child coroutines have finished executing, offering a structured and predictable execution flow.

To dive deeper, let's examine the fundamental aspects of coroutine scopes and structured concurrency:

- **Global Scope** - Although not recommended for structured concurrency due to its potential to lead to leaks and uncontrolled execution, GlobalScope is available for launching coroutines that live for the entire application lifecycle.

- **CoroutineScope** - A general-purpose scope that can be created providing a CoroutineContext. This scope is used for launch-

182

ing coroutines in a structured manner within a specific context, ensuring controlled execution.

- **ViewModelScope** - Specific to Android development, viewModelScope is an extension property available in a ViewModel. Kotlin coroutines launched in this scope are automatically canceled when the ViewModel is cleared.

- **LifecycleScope** - Another scope specific to Android development, lifecycleScope is used to launch coroutines in a lifecycle-aware manner. Coroutines in this scope are canceled when the lifecycle is destroyed.

To illustrate how structured concurrency is used in Kotlin, consider the following example:

```
import kotlinx.coroutines.*

fun main() {
    runBlocking {
        launch {
            delay(1000L)
            println("Task from runBlocking")
        }

        coroutineScope {
            launch {
                delay(500L)
                println("Task from nested launch")
            }
            delay(100L)
            println("Task from coroutineScope")
        }

        println("Coroutine scope is over")
    }
}
```

In this example:

- runBlocking provides a blocking coroutine scope for the main coroutine, ensuring the application does not exit before the coroutine completes.

- Within runBlocking, a coroutineScope block is defined. It creates a new scope without blocking the current thread. It ensures that all the coroutines launched within this scope must complete before proceeding.

- Two nested coroutines are launched, one directly within runBlocking and another inside the coroutineScope. The nested launch will wait for both coroutines to complete due to structured concurrency.

The result of this code execution demonstrates structured concurrency in action:

```
Task from coroutineScope
Task from nested launch
Task from runBlocking
Coroutine scope is over
```

The output order is determined by delays and the structured nature of the concurrent tasks. This example highlights how Kotlin's coroutine scopes facilitate structured concurrency, ensuring predictable and manageable asynchronous executions.

Exception Handling in Structured Concurrency

One of the advantages of structured concurrency is its approach to exception handling. An uncaught exception in any coroutine within a scope will cause the scope to be cancelled, which in turn cancels all coroutines launched in that scope. This behavior ensures that an error in one part of the concurrent execution graph does not leave the application in an inconsistent state.

Consider the following example demonstrating exception handling within structured concurrency:

```
1  import kotlinx.coroutines.*
2
3  fun main() = runBlocking {
4      val scope = CoroutineScope(Job())
5
6      scope.launch {
```

```
7      delay(200L)
8      throw RuntimeException("Error in coroutine")
9    }
10
11   scope.launch {
12       delay(500L)
13       println("Second coroutine is cancelled due to an error in the
             first one.")
14   }
15
16   delay(Long.MAX_VALUE)
17  }
```

This sample illustrates how an exception in one coroutine leads to the cancellation of the entire scope, including all coroutines launched within it. Exception handling in structured concurrency ensures that errors are propagated and managed cohesively across coroutine hierarchies, further enhancing the robustness and reliability of concurrent Kotlin applications.

7.6   Suspending Functions: The Basics

Suspending functions are a cornerstone of Kotlin's coroutine mechanism, allowing for non-blocking asynchronous programming. A suspending function, as implied by the name, can be suspended by the coroutine at a certain point without blocking the thread on which the coroutine is running. This feature is critical for writing efficient and responsive applications, especially those involving IO operations or complex computations that can benefit from concurrency.

To declare a suspending function in Kotlin, the suspend modifier is used. This modifier can be applied to any function, indicating that the function can suspend execution without blocking. Here's a basic example:

```
1  suspend fun fetchData(): String {
2      // Simulate a long-running operation
3      delay(1000L) // Delays are non-blocking
4      return "Data fetched"
5  }
```

In the example above, delay(1000L) is a suspending function provided by Kotlin's Standard Library. It simulates a time-consuming operation, such as fetching data from a database or a remote server, without blocking. However, it's important to note that suspending functions like fetchData() can only be called from coroutines or other suspending functions. Attempting to call them directly from non-suspending code will result in a compilation error.

The power of suspending functions lies in their ability to pause and resume their execution. When a coroutine reaches a suspending call, it suspends its execution. The underlying thread is released back to the coroutine's dispatcher, which can use it to run other coroutines or tasks. Once the suspending call completes, the coroutine resumes its execution from the point of suspension.

To illustrate this, consider the following code snippet that launches a coroutine to call fetchData():

```
1  fun main() = runBlocking {
2      launch {
3          val result = fetchData()
4          println(result)
5      }
6  }
```

The launch builder starts a new coroutine that calls fetchData(). Despite the delay, the main thread is not blocked by the suspending function, which showcases the non-blocking nature of suspending functions.

Coroutines can leverage multiple suspending functions to perform complex asynchronous operations in a sequential manner:

```
1   suspend fun processData(data: String): String {
2       delay(500L) // Another non-blocking delay
3       return "Processed $data"
4   }
5
6   fun main() = runBlocking {
7       launch {
8           val fetchedData = fetchData()
9           val processedData = processData(fetchedData)
10          println(processedData)
```

186

```
11        }
12  }
```

In the modified example, the coroutine sequentially calls two
suspending functions: `fetchData()` and `processData()`. The
coroutine is suspended twice without blocking the main thread,
demonstrating how suspending functions can be composed and
executed in sequence for complex asynchronous workflows.

Suspending functions are not just limited to returning a simple result. They can also return other types, such as `Deferred<T>` when
used with the `async` builder for concurrent operations, or emit multiple values over time when used with Kotlin's `Flow` API. These advanced use cases further extend the flexibility and power of suspending functions in Kotlin coroutines.

Understanding and effectively using suspending functions is
essential for maximizing the potential of Kotlin's concurrency
model.   By enabling efficient, non-blocking asynchronous
operations, suspending functions lay the foundation for responsive
and performant Kotlin applications.

7.7   Coroutine Context and Dispatchers

In this section, we will discuss the critical concepts of coroutine context and dispatchers within the Kotlin programming language. Understanding these concepts is essential for effectively managing concurrent tasks and their execution threads in Kotlin applications.

Coroutine context is a set of various elements that define the
behavior of a coroutine. It includes details such as the coroutine's
job, dispatcher, and any additional information relevant to its
execution, such as custom elements defined by the developer. One
of the key components of the coroutine context is the
CoroutineDispatcher, which determines what thread or threads the
corresponding coroutine uses for its execution.

Understanding CoroutineDispatcher

CoroutineDispatcher controls the thread that a coroutine uses to execute its task. Kotlin provides several dispatcher options that cater to
different use cases:

- `Dispatchers.Default` – This dispatcher is optimized for CPU-
  intensive work. It utilises a shared background pool of threads.

- `Dispatchers.IO` – Optimized for IO-intensive tasks, this
  dispatcher uses a shared pool of threads designed to handle
  input/output operations like reading or writing to the file
  system, databases, or networking.

- `Dispatchers.Main` – This dispatcher is confined to the main
  thread of the application, making it suitable for interacting with
  the UI or performing quick tasks.

- `Dispatchers.Unconfined` – A special dispatcher that starts
  the coroutine in the caller thread but allows it to resume in
  whichever thread that is available when the suspension
  occurs. This dispatcher is not recommended for general use.

Setting the Coroutine Context

To set the coroutine context, one can specify the dispatcher when
launching a coroutine. The following example demonstrates the use
of different dispatchers:

```
1   import kotlinx.coroutines.*
2
3   fun main() = runBlocking {
4
5       launch(Dispatchers.Default) {
6           println("Default dispatcher. Thread: ${Thread.currentThread().
                name}")
7       }
8
9       launch(Dispatchers.IO) {
10          println("IO dispatcher. Thread: ${Thread.currentThread().name}")
```

```
11    }
12
13    launch(Dispatchers.Main) {
14        println("Main dispatcher. Thread: ${Thread.currentThread().name}
              ")
15    }
16
17    launch(Dispatchers.Unconfined) {
18        println("Unconfined dispatcher. Thread: ${Thread.currentThread()
              .name}")
19    }
20 }
```

The output of such a program demonstrates how each coroutine runs
on a thread corresponding to its dispatcher:

```
Default dispatcher. Thread: DefaultDispatcher-worker-1
IO dispatcher. Thread: DefaultDispatcher-worker-2
Main dispatcher. Thread: Main
Unconfined dispatcher. Thread: main
```

In addition to choosing a dispatcher, a coroutine's context can be further customized by adding elements such as CoroutineName or combining multiple contexts using the plus (+) operator. For instance, to
combine a dispatcher with a custom name for the coroutine, the following syntax is used:

```
1 launch(Dispatchers.Default + CoroutineName("MyCoroutine")) {
2     println("Running in ${coroutineContext[CoroutineName.Key]}")
3 }
```

Understanding and effectively utilizing coroutine contexts and
dispatchers allow developers to achieve precise control over
coroutine execution, facilitating the creation of highly responsive
and efficient Kotlin applications. Through strategic choice and
customization of coroutine contexts, tasks can be executed on
appropriate threads, thus optimizing the application's performance
and responsiveness.

189

7.8   Combining Coroutines: Sequential and Parallel Execution

Combining coroutines efficiently to achieve both sequential and parallel execution is essential for optimizing the responsiveness and throughput of Kotlin applications. This section examines strategies for structuring coroutine execution in both manners, leveraging the flexibility and power of Kotlin's concurrency model.

Sequential Execution with Coroutines

Sequential execution in the context of coroutines refers to the initiation of one coroutine after the completion of another. This pattern is particularly useful for tasks that must be executed in a specific order where the output or side effect of one task is a prerequisite for the start of the next.

To achieve sequential execution, one could use the `async` builder along with the `await` function. The following example illustrates this concept:

```
suspend fun firstTask(): Int {
    delay(1000) // Simulates a computation or IO delay
    return 10
}

suspend fun secondTask(input: Int): Int {
    delay(1000) // Simulates a computation or IO delay
    return input * 2
}

fun main() = runBlocking<Unit> {
    val firstResult = async { firstTask() }
    val secondResult = async { secondTask(firstResult.await()) }
    println("Total: ${secondResult.await()}")
}
```

In the example above, `secondTask` commences only after the completion of `firstTask`, demonstrating sequential execution within the coroutine context.

Parallel Execution with Coroutines

Parallel execution, in contrast, involves running multiple coroutines simultaneously, thus not waiting for one to finish before starting another. This pattern is especially beneficial for independent tasks that do not require the results of one another to proceed.

Parallel execution can also be achieved using the async builder, but with a slight modification to ensure that the coroutines run in parallel:

```
1   suspend fun taskOne(): Int {
2       delay(1000) // Simulates a computation or IO delay
3       return 20
4   }
5
6   suspend fun taskTwo(): Int {
7       delay(1000) // Simulates a computation or IO delay
8       return 40
9   }
10
11  fun main() = runBlocking<Unit> {
12      val resultOne = async { taskOne() }
13      val resultTwo = async { taskTwo() }
14      println("Combined Result: ${resultOne.await() + resultTwo.await()}"
            )
15  }
```

In the parallel execution example, taskOne and taskTwo commence almost simultaneously, illustrating the power of coroutines to perform concurrent operations with minimal syntactic overhead.

Choosing Between Sequential and Parallel Execution

The choice between sequential and parallel execution depends largely on the nature of the tasks at hand. If tasks are dependent, requiring the output of a preceding operation, sequential execution is appropriate. Conversely, if tasks can proceed independently without waiting for the results of others, parallel execution can significantly reduce overall execution time and increase application throughput.

Moreover, it is possible to combine sequential and parallel executions within a single coroutine scope to leverage the strengths of both patterns. Carefully structuring these executions allows developers the flexibility to optimize performance and responsiveness in Kotlin applications.

This detailed exploration of combining coroutines for sequential and parallel execution underscores the versatility and power of Kotlin's concurrency model, enabling developers to write more efficient and responsive applications.

7.9   Error Handling in Coroutines

Error handling in coroutines is a crucial aspect of writing robust and resilient Kotlin applications. In traditional, synchronous code, exceptions are handled using the try-catch blocks. Kotlin coroutines extend this model, offering structured concurrency principles that simplify error handling in asynchronous operations. Understanding how to effectively manage errors in a coroutine context is paramount to leveraging the full power of Kotlin's concurrency model.

Firstly, it's essential to recognize that exceptions in coroutines propagate in a specific manner, depending on the coroutine builder used and the structure of the coroutine hierarchy. Two primary coroutine builders, `launch` and `async`, exhibit different behaviors in error handling.

- The `launch` builder will propagate exceptions to the global coroutine exception handler if not caught locally within the coroutine. It's designed for fire-and-forget tasks, where the primary concern is to execute a task asynchronously.

- The `async` builder, however, encapsulates the exception in the resulting `Deferred` object. To handle the exception, one must explicitly await the result and use a try-catch block.

Consider the following example illustrating error propagation using the `launch` builder:

```
1   import kotlinx.coroutines.*
2
3   fun main() = runBlocking {
4       val job = launch {
5           throw IllegalArgumentException("Invalid argument")
6       }
7       try {
8           job.join()
9       } catch (e: IllegalStateException) {
10          println("Caught $e")
11      }
12  }
```

In the example above, the exception thrown within the `launch` coroutine is caught in the global exception handler. This illustrates the default behavior of uncaught exceptions propagating through the coroutine hierarchy.

Next, observe the error handling with the `async` builder:

```
1   import kotlinx.coroutines.*
2
3   fun main() = runBlocking {
4       val deferred = async {
5           throw IllegalArgumentException("Invalid argument")
6       }
7       try {
8           deferred.await()
9       } catch (e: IllegalArgumentException) {
10          println("Caught $e")
11      }
12  }
```

Here, the `async` coroutine encapsulates the exception, allowing it to be handled explicitly when the result is awaited. This demonstrates the encapsulation behavior of the `async` builder in regards to exceptions.

Coroutine context and dispatchers also play a significant role in error handling. The `CoroutineExceptionHandler` context element is particularly useful for globally handling uncaught exceptions in coroutines. This handler is invoked if an exception is not caught locally within the coroutine.

```kotlin
import kotlinx.coroutines.*

val handler = CoroutineExceptionHandler { _, exception ->
    println("Caught $exception")
}

fun main() = runBlocking {
    val job = launch(handler) {
        throw IllegalArgumentException("Invalid argument")
    }
    job.join()
}
```

In the code snippet above, `CoroutineExceptionHandler` is specified as part of the coroutine context in `launch`. This handler catches any exceptions not caught within the coroutine itself, demonstrating a global approach to error handling in coroutines.

Finally, it's important to emphasize structured concurrency in Kotlin, which mandates that a coroutine must complete all its children before completing itself. This ensures a predictable and reliable error propagation mechanism, where the parent coroutine can handle exceptions from its children coroutines effectively.

In summary, error handling in Kotlin coroutines involves understanding the behavior of coroutine builders, the role of coroutine context, and the principle of structured concurrency for predictable exception propagation. By effectively managing exceptions in coroutines, developers can ensure the resilience and robustness of their Kotlin applications.

7.10   Flow: Handling Streams of Data

In this section, we will discuss Kotlin's Flow API which is a crucial component when dealing with streams of data asynchronously. The Flow API is part of Kotlin's coroutines and is designed for handling a sequence of data that is asynchronously computed. This means that rather than blocking the main thread until all the data is available, data is emitted and can be processed as soon as it becomes available, enhancing the application's responsiveness.

To begin with, the basic syntax for defining a Flow in Kotlin is as follows:

```
import kotlinx.coroutines.*
import kotlinx.coroutines.flow.*

fun simpleFlow(): Flow<Int> = flow {
    for (i in 1..3) {
        delay(100) // Mimic a long-running asynchronous operation
        emit(i) // Emit the next value
    }
}
```

In the above example, the `simpleFlow` function returns a Flow of integers. The `flow` builder is used to define a sequence of integers from 1 to 3, with a 100ms delay between each emission to mimic an asynchronous operation. The `emit` function is used within the flow builder to send out (or "emit") values one at a time.

To collect or consume the values emitted by a Flow, we use the `collect` function, typically within a coroutine scope, as Flow collections are asynchronous operations:

```
fun main() = runBlocking<Unit> {
    launch {
        simpleFlow().collect { value ->
            println(value)
        }
    }
}
```

Upon executing this program, the following output is observed:

```
1
2
3
```

This indicates that each value is printed to the console as it is emitted from the Flow, following the artificial delay.

It is important to distinguish between cold and hot streams. Flows in Kotlin are cold streams, meaning that the code inside a Flow builder does not run until the flow is collected. This behavior is different from hot streams which start emitting values immediately upon creation, regardless of whether there are any collectors.

Flows also support various intermediate and terminal operators for transforming and combining data streams. For example, the map operator can be used to transform each emitted value:

```
fun mappedFlow(): Flow<String> = simpleFlow().map { value ->
    "Value is $value" // Transform Int to String
}
```

Another powerful feature of Flow is its built-in support for backpressure, denoting the ability to handle scenarios where data is produced faster than it can be consumed. Flow handles backpressure implicitly by suspending emission of values until the current value is processed by the collector, thus providing a robust mechanism for dealing with streams of data in an efficient and responsive manner.

In summary, Kotlin's Flow API extends the capabilities of coroutine-based asynchronous programming by enabling the processing of streams of data efficiently and responsively. Its integration into the coroutine ecosystem allows for a seamless development experience when handling asynchronous streams, making Flow an indispensable tool for Kotlin developers working with real-time data.

7.11 Cancellation and Timeouts in Coroutines

Cancellation and timeouts are essential concepts within coroutine-based asynchronous programming in Kotlin. They allow developers to write responsive applications that can terminate operations that are no longer needed or that take too long to complete. Understanding how to effectively manage cancellation and timeouts is crucial for creating robust and efficient applications.

Cancellation in Coroutines

Kotlin coroutines are cooperative by nature. This means a coroutine must cooperate in its own cancellation. The coroutine's job facilitates this process, offering a way to cancel the execution of the coroutine. However, it is the responsibility of the coroutine's code to check for cancellation and respond appropriately.

To initiate cancellation, the cancel() method is called on the coroutine's Job. For example:

```
1  val job = launch {
2      // Coroutine's work
3  }
4  job.cancel()
```

To make a coroutine cancellable, it needs to periodically check for its cancellation status. This can be achieved using the isActive property, which is a part of the CoroutineScope. Alternatively, suspending functions like yield() and delay() automatically check for cancellation and throw a CancellationException when they detect cancellation.

```
1  val job = launch {
2      while(isActive) { // Checks for cancellation
3          // Perform work
4      }
5  }
```

Additionally, manual checks can be inserted by using the ensureActive() method, which throws a CancellationException if the coroutine has been cancelled.

Timeouts

Timeouts are a special case of cancellation. Kotlin provides the withTimeout() and withTimeoutOrNull() functions to support timeout operations. If the operation within the timeout block does not complete within the specified time limit, withTimeout() throws a TimeoutCancellationException, effectively canceling the coroutine.

On the other hand, `withTimeoutOrNull()` returns null instead of throwing an exception.

Example using `withTimeout()`:

```
1  try {
2      withTimeout(1000L) { // Timeout of 1000ms
3          // Perform operation that might take longer than 1000ms
4      }
5  } catch(e: TimeoutCancellationException) {
6      println("Operation timed out")
7  }
```

For situations where throwing an exception is not desirable, `withTimeoutOrNull()` can be used as follows:

```
1  val result = withTimeoutOrNull(1000L) { // Timeout of 1000ms
2      // Perform operation
3      "Finished" // Return value
4  }
5  if (result == null) {
6      println("Operation timed out and returned null")
7  }
```

In practice, handling timeouts gracefully allows applications to avoid wasting resources on operations that exceed their expected duration, thus maintaining responsiveness and efficiency.

Best Practices

When implementing cancellation and timeouts, consider the following best practices:

- Regularly check for cancellation in long-running or computationally intensive coroutines.

- Use `withTimeoutOrNull()` for non-critical timeouts where an operation can safely be skipped if it takes too long.

- Handle `TimeoutCancellationException` to clean up resources or rollback changes if necessary.

- Avoid excessive granularity in checking for cancellation to prevent introducing unnecessary overhead.

By adhering to these practices, developers can ensure that their Kotlin coroutines behave predictably under various conditions, contributing to the overall robustness and usability of their applications.

7.12 Advanced Coroutine Use Cases and Patterns

Coroutines in Kotlin introduce an efficient way of managing asynchronous tasks, significantly simplifying code that would otherwise be cumbersome with traditional threading mechanisms. This section explores advanced use cases and design patterns leveraging Kotlin coroutines, offering insight into their powerful capabilities in complex real-world scenarios.

Combining Network Requests

One common scenario in modern application development involves combining data from multiple network requests. With coroutines, this can be achieved with a higher level of readability and efficiency. Consider a use case where we need to fetch user details and their posts from separate API endpoints concurrently and then combine the results:

```
suspend fun fetchUserDataAndPosts(): Pair<User, List<Post>> =
    coroutineScope {
    val userDeferred = async { api.fetchUserDetails() }
    val postsDeferred = async { api.fetchUserPosts() }
    Pair(userDeferred.await(), postsDeferred.await())
}
```

In the above example, async is used to initiate concurrent requests. await() suspends the function until its respective task completes, ensuring that both requests are completed before combining their results.

Resource Cleanup with `try` and `finally`

Managing resources in asynchronous programming is crucial to prevent leaks and ensure proper cleanup. Coroutines provide a structured way to handle resources with `try` and `finally` blocks. Consider a case where we open a file and ensure it's closed after processing, even if an exception occurs:

```
1  suspend fun readFileContent(path: String): String = coroutineScope {
2      val file = openFile(path)
3      try {
4          // Operations on the file
5      } finally {
6          file.close()
7      }
8  }
```

This pattern guarantees the file is closed by placing `file.close()` within the `finally` block, preserving resource integrity even in the face of errors.

Exponential Backoff Strategy

Retry strategies are fundamental in dealing with transient failures in network requests or remote procedure calls. An exponential backoff strategy, where the wait time between retries exponentially increases, can be elegantly implemented with coroutines:

```
1   suspend fun <T> retryWithExponentialBackoff(
2       maxAttempts: Int = 3,
3       initialDelay: Long = 100,
4       maxDelay: Long = 10000,
5       operation: suspend () -> T
6   ): T {
7       var currentDelay = initialDelay
8       repeat(maxAttempts) {
9           try {
10              return operation()
```

```
11        } catch (e: Exception) {
12            if (it == maxAttempts - 1) throw e
13            delay(currentDelay)
14            currentDelay = (currentDelay * 2).coerceAtMost(maxDelay)
15        }
16    }
17    throw IllegalArgumentException("Reached max retry attempts")
18 }
```

In this pattern, delay() is used to suspend the coroutine without blocking, allowing for a non-blocking exponential backoff mechanism.

Flow Control with Channels

Channels provide a way to communicate between coroutines, supporting different patterns of usage such as fan-out, fan-in, and pipeline processing. Here is an example of a simple pipeline processing pattern:

```
1  suspend fun produceNumbers() = produce<Int> {
2      for (x in 1..5) {
3          send(x)
4      }
5  }
6
7  suspend fun squareNumbers(numbers: ReceiveChannel<Int>) = produce<Int>
       {
8      for (x in numbers) {
9          send(x * x)
10     }
11 }
```

In this pipeline, produceNumbers() generates numbers which are then squared by squareNumbers(). Channels facilitate this producer-consumer pattern, showcasing a structured approach to flow control in concurrent operations.

These advanced patterns elucidate the versatility and power of Kotlin coroutines in managing complex asynchronous tasks. Understanding these patterns equips developers with the tools needed to tackle real-world challenges effectively, making the most of Kotlin's cutting-edge coroutine support.

Chapter 8

Interoperability with Java

This chapter addresses Kotlin's seamless interoperability with Java, a critical feature that allows developers to integrate Kotlin into existing Java codebases without rewriting applications from scratch. It provides a comprehensive guide on how to call Java code from Kotlin and vice versa, handling nullability in interoperable scenarios, and utilizing Java collections within Kotlin applications. Additionally, it highlights the use of annotations and generics across the two languages, ensuring a smooth transition and efficient coexistence. Through practical examples and best practices, readers will learn how to leverage the strengths of both languages within their projects, maximizing productivity and application performance.

8.1 Introduction to Kotlin-Java Interoperability

Interoperability between Kotlin and Java stands as a cornerstone feature of the Kotlin programming language. Given that Kotlin operates on the Java Virtual Machine (JVM), it is designed from the ground up to be fully interoperable with Java. This interoperable nature enables developers to utilize Kotlin in conjunction with existing Java codebases, facilitating a smooth integration process without the need for rewriting applications.

The primary objective of this interoperability is to leverage the strengths of both languages within a single project. Kotlin offers concise syntax and advanced features such as null safety, while Java is known for its robust ecosystem and comprehensive libraries. By allowing these two languages to operate together seamlessly, developers can enhance productivity and application performance.

Let's discuss the procedural aspects of calling Java from Kotlin. When Kotlin code interacts with Java, it does so in a straightforward manner. Kotlin automatically recognizes Java libraries and allows them to be called as if they were native Kotlin functions. This is achieved through Kotlin's inbuilt type inference mechanism, which understands Java types and translates them into their Kotlin equivalents. Importantly, when integrating Java code, issues related to null safety and platform types must be considered to prevent null pointer exceptions.

In turn, calling Kotlin from Java is equally straightforward. Kotlin compiles down to Java byte code, making all Kotlin functions accessible to Java. Kotlin class files include metadata that allows Java to recognize and use Kotlin-specific features such as properties, default parameter values, and extension functions. However, some Kotlin features, like extension functions and properties, require the use of generated Java class methods to be accessed from Java code, as Java does not natively support these constructs.

Interoperability also extends to handling nullability. Kotlin's type system distinguishes between nullable and non-nullable types, enforcing strict null checks at compile-time to prevent null pointer exceptions. When interacting with Java, which has no concept of null safety, Kotlin treats Java types as nullable, thereby requiring developers to perform explicit null checks or assertions when using Java objects in Kotlin code.

Another important aspect of interoperability involves using Java collections in Kotlin. Kotlin extends Java's collection framework, providing additional functional-style operations and ensuring null safety when accessing collection elements. Despite these enhancements, Java collections can be directly accessed and manipulated within Kotlin code, allowing for the use of familiar Java-based collection APIs alongside Kotlin's own improvements.

Java generics and Kotlin type parameters also demonstrate interoperability. Kotlin's type parameters work seamlessly with Java's generics, enabling the use of generic Java classes within Kotlin. However, due to type erasure in Java, some issues can arise when using generic types that Kotlin can infer at compile-time but which are erased at runtime in Java. These issues are typically addressed through the use of explicit type casts and annotations in Kotlin to preserve type information.

The use of interoperable naming through the @JvmName annotation provides a means to resolve naming conflicts that may arise between Kotlin and Java. This annotation allows developers to specify an alternative name for a Kotlin function or property when it is called from Java, thereby avoiding name clashes with existing Java methods or reserved keywords.

Creating Kotlin extensions for Java classes illustrates the powerful synergy between Kotlin and Java. Extension functions in Kotlin enable developers to add new functionality to existing Java classes without modifying their source code. These extensions are statically resolved, meaning they do not alter the class's inheritance tree, making them an ideal tool for enhancing Java classes with Kotlin's expressive syntax and additional functionalities.

Working with Kotlin and Java annotations showcases the compatibility of annotation processing between the two languages. Kotlin fully supports Java annotations, allowing them to be used on Kotlin declarations. Similarly, Kotlin annotations can be utilized in Java, provided they are marked with the @Retention and @Target meta-annotations specifying their retention policy and applicable targets.

Kotlin-Java interoperability is a highly beneficial feature that significantly enhances the flexibility and efficiency of developing applications on the JVM. Through careful handling of nullability, use of Java collections, integration of generics, and strategic application of annotations, developers can effectively leverage the strengths of both Kotlin and Java in their projects. The following sections will delve into these aspects in greater detail, providing practical examples and best practices for achieving seamless interoperability.

8.2   Calling Java from Kotlin

In this section, we discuss the seamless mechanism that Kotlin provides for calling Java code, encompassing everything from invoking Java methods, accessing fields, and instantiating Java classes. This interoperability is fundamental to Kotlin's design and facilitates integrating Kotlin into existing Java codebases.

Kotlin treats Java types as if they were native Kotlin types, and this applies to both Java classes and interfaces. However, certain differences in language features and null safety require special attention. Let's explore the specifics through detailed examples and explanations.

Accessing Java Methods and Fields

Kotlin enables direct access to Java methods and fields as if they were part of Kotlin classes. Consider a Java class named JavaExample with a method printMessage() and a field message.

```
1  public class JavaExample {
2      public String message = "Hello from Java!";
3
4      public void printMessage() {
5          System.out.println(message);
6      }
7  }
```

Accessing this method and field from Kotlin is straightforward:

```
1  fun main() {
2      val javaExample = JavaExample()
```

206

```
3      println(javaExample.message) // Accessing field
4      javaExample.printMessage() // Calling method
5    }
```

Handling Nullability

One of the fundamental differences between Kotlin and Java is Kotlin's strict null safety. When calling Java code from Kotlin, the Kotlin compiler does not have information about the nullability of Java types. As a result, Kotlin treats Java types as platform types, denoted by 'ᵢ, which accepts both nullable and non-nullable assignments. This flexibility comes with the responsibility of handling potential 'NullPointerExceptions'.

For instance, if the JavaExample class returned a String that could potentially be null:

```
1  public class JavaExample {
2      public String getMessage() {
3          // This might return null
4          return null;
5      }
6  }
```

Kotlin code needs to check for nullability to avoid runtime exceptions:

```
1  fun main() {
2      val javaExample = JavaExample()
3      val message = javaExample.getMessage()
4      println(message?.length ?: "The string is null")
5  }
```

Instantiating Java Classes

Creating instances of Java classes in Kotlin does not require the 'new' keyword, aligning with Kotlin's constructor call syntax. This simplification streamlines code, making it more concise and readable:

```
1  val javaExample = JavaExample() // No `new` keyword needed
```

207

Java Static Methods and Fields

Kotlin accesses Java static methods and fields through the companion object of the Java class, leveraging Kotlin's object-oriented features to interact with Java's static context. Consider a Java class with a static method and field:

```
1  public class JavaStatics {
2      public static String staticField = "Static field in Java";
3
4      public static void staticMethod() {
5          System.out.println("Static method in Java");
6      }
7  }
```

Kotlin accesses these static members directly through the Java class name:

```
1  fun main() {
2      println(JavaStatics.staticField) // Accessing static field
3      JavaStatics.staticMethod() // Calling static method
4  }
```

This section has detailed how Kotlin makes calling Java code straightforward, akin to using Kotlin-native types, whilst highlighting key areas requiring careful consideration, especially nullability and static member access. The next sections will delve into the inverse scenario, elucidating how Java code can effectively call Kotlin, managing Kotlin features that Java lacks, such as property accessors, extension functions, and null-safety annotations.

8.3   Calling Kotlin from Java

Calling Kotlin code from Java is as straightforward as invoking Java code from Kotlin, thanks to the interoperability features designed into Kotlin. This interoperability is not incidental but a core design feature of Kotlin, enabling developers to utilize Kotlin's advanced features while maintaining their existing Java codebase.   This section elaborates on the essential aspects and specific steps involved in invoking Kotlin functions and accessing Kotlin properties from Java code, providing clear examples to ensure comprehensive understanding.

When Kotlin compiles its code, it is translated into bytecode that runs on the Java Virtual Machine (JVM), making the compiled Kotlin code essentially indistinguishable from Java bytecode. This design choice facilitates the seamless callability of Kotlin code from Java. However, there are notable differences in how Kotlin handles certain constructs, such as properties, null safety, and default arguments, which require special consideration when calling from Java.

Accessing Kotlin Properties

Kotlin properties are accessed from Java code as if they were Java fields. However, under the hood, Kotlin properties are compiled to getter and setter methods. Let's consider a Kotlin class with a property:

```
1   class SampleClass(val data: String)
```

From Java, this property is accessed through the automatically generated getData() method:

```
1   SampleClass sample = new SampleClass("Hello, Kotlin!");
2   String data = sample.getData();
```

While the Kotlin side maintains property syntax, Java accesses these as methods, following the JavaBean convention.

Calling Kotlin Functions

Kotlin functions are called from Java in a manner similar to Java methods. Given a Kotlin function:

```
1   fun sayHello(name: String): String {
2       return "Hello, $name"
3   }
```

209

The corresponding Java call is straightforward:

```
1   String greeting = MyClassKt.sayHello("Java");
```

Note the use of MyClassKt; Kotlin functions declared in a file are placed in a class named after the filename, suffixed with Kt. This class does not exist in the Kotlin code but is generated by the Kotlin compiler for use in Java.

Handling Nullability

Kotlin's null safety features introduce considerations when calling Kotlin from Java, given Java's lack of null safety.   For interoperability, Kotlin types are seen from Java as nullable or not based on annotations:

- If a Kotlin parameter, function, or property is explicitly marked with @Nullable, Java treats it as nullable.

- Conversely, if marked with @NotNull, it is treated as non-nullable in Java.

Ignoring these annotations can lead to NullPointerExceptions at runtime, highlighting the importance of adhering to Kotlin's nullability when interacting from Java.

Utilizing Default Arguments and Named Parameters

One of Kotlin's conveniences is the ability to define default values for function parameters and to use named parameters for clearer calls.   When calling such a Kotlin function from Java, every parameter must be specified, and named parameters are not supported due to Java's language limitations. For Kotlin functions with default arguments wishing to maintain these defaults when called from Java, the @JvmOverloads annotation can be used in Kotlin, which instructs the Kotlin compiler to generate overloaded methods for Java to call:

```
1   @JvmOverloads
2   fun greet(greeting: String = "Hello", name: String = "world") {
3       println("$greeting, $name")
4   }
```

This Kotlin function compiles to several Java methods, enabling Java code to call it with any number of arguments:

```
1   GreetingKt.greet();
2   GreetingKt.greet("Hi");
3   GreetingKt.greet("Hi", "Kotlin");
```

These examples illustrate the fundamentals of calling Kotlin from Java, emphasizing the ease with which developers can integrate Kotlin into existing Java applications. While certain Kotlin features require special consideration when accessed from Java, the Kotlin team has made significant efforts to ensure that these interactions are as smooth and intuitive as possible. Understanding these interoperability patterns enables developers to leverage the full power of both Kotlin and Java in their applications.

8.4   Handling Nullability in Kotlin and Java

One of the pivotal aspects of Kotlin-Java interoperability involves handling nullability. Nullability is a concept that denotes whether a variable can hold a null value. Kotlin's type system is designed to eliminate the dreaded NullPointerException at compile-time through null safety. However, Java, being an older language, does not have such a strong type system to prevent nulls. Therefore, when Kotlin code calls Java code or vice versa, understanding how nullability is managed between the two languages is crucial.

Kotlin distinguishes between nullable and non-nullable types. A non-nullable type cannot hold a null value, ensuring safer code. However, when Kotlin interacts with Java, the Java code's nullability annotations are taken into account. Java's annotations such as @Nullable and @NonNull inform the Kotlin compiler about the nullability of Java types.

```
 1   // Example of Java method
 2   @Nullable
 3   public String getNullableString() {
 4       return null;
 5   }
 6
 7   @NonNull
 8   public String getNonNullString() {
 9       return "A Non-Null String";
10   }
```

When calling these methods from Kotlin, the compiler uses the annotations to infer the nullability of the methods' return types.

```
 1   val nullableString: String? = JavaClass().getNullableString()
 2   val nonNullString: String = JavaClass().getNonNullString()
```

In the above example, the Kotlin compiler correctly infers nullableString as a nullable type (String?) and nonNullString as a non-nullable type (String).

Conversely, when Java code calls Kotlin functions, the Kotlin compiler generates nullability annotations for Java to interpret. This conversion ensures that Java code can safely interact with Kotlin without risking a NullPointerException.

```
 1   // Kotlin function
 2   fun getNullableKotlinString(): String? = null
```

This Kotlin function will have a nullability annotation when viewed from Java:

```
@Nullable
public String getNullableKotlinString() {
    return null;
}
```

However, a noteworthy complication arises when Java code does not use nullability annotations. Kotlin offers a solution referred to as platform types, denoted by a single exclamation mark (String!). Platform types allow the Kotlin compiler to delegate the responsibility of null checking to the developer, reflecting the inherently nullable nature of Java types.

```
1  // Calling a Java method without nullability annotations
2  val unknownNullabilityString: String! = JavaClass().
       getStringWithoutAnnotation()
```

In this case, the Kotlin developer must explicitly manage the nullability through checks or assertions.

To further refine interoperability, Kotlin provides the @JvmField and @JvmOverloads annotations, allowing for seamless usage of Kotlin properties and methods with default parameters in Java, respectively.

In summary, handling nullability in Kotlin and Java interoperability is facilitated through careful use of nullability annotations and the strategic employment of platform types. These mechanisms ensure that the integration of Kotlin into Java codebases, and vice versa, does not compromise the safety and robustness of the application.

8.5 Using Java Collections in Kotlin

Kotlin treats Java collections as part of its standard library due to its inherent interoperability with Java. However, the Kotlin standard library adds extension functions that enable more idiomatic usage of these collections within Kotlin code. This characteristic is crucial for developers working on projects that involve both Kotlin and Java codebases, enabling them to utilize the vast array of Java libraries and frameworks without sacrificing the conciseness and expressiveness of Kotlin.

The primary distinction between Java and Kotlin collections lies in Kotlin's handling of mutability. In Java, collections are inherently mutable, with immutable collections being a relatively recent addition requiring explicit declarations or usage of third-party libraries. On the other hand, Kotlin distinguishes between mutable and immutable collections at the language level, allowing developers to express intent more clearly and enforce immutability where applicable.

To use Java collections in Kotlin effectively, it's essential to understand how Kotlin classifies these collections and the implications for code interoperability and safety.

- **Read-Only and Mutable Collections**: Kotlin manifests collections as either read-only or mutable. This is not an enforcement of immutability at the runtime level, but a compile-time distinction that promotes immutable design patterns.

- **Automatic Conversion**: When calling a Java method that returns a collection from Kotlin, Kotlin does not distinguish between mutable and immutable collections.

Let's consider an example where we call Java code that returns a `java.util.List` from Kotlin:

```
fun getJavaList(): List<String> {
    return JavaCollectionsClass.getMutableList()
}
```

Here, `JavaCollectionsClass.getMutableList()` returns a `java.util.List` instance, which Kotlin treats as a read-only `List`. It's crucial to remember that this does not convert the collection into an immutable one; the underlying collection is still mutable, but Kotlin's type system prevents modification through Kotlin code.

To modify such collections, they must be explicitly declared as mutable in Kotlin:

```
fun modifyJavaList() {
    val mutableList: MutableList<String> = JavaCollectionsClass.
        getMutableList() as MutableList<String>
    mutableList.add("New Element")
}
```

This snippet showcases the casting of the Java collection to Kotlin's `MutableList`, allowing modification operations. This interoperability feature is a double-edged sword; it provides flexibility and ensures that Kotlin can work seamlessly with Java's mutable collections, but it also introduces the potential for runtime errors if the collection is not inherently mutable.

Handling nullability is another critical aspect when working with Java collections in Kotlin, as Java's type system does not enforce null safety.

Consider the following Java method:

```
public List<String> getStrings() {
    return new ArrayList<>(Arrays.asList("Hello", null, "World"));
}
```

When this method is called from Kotlin, the type inferred by the compiler is List<String?>, reflecting that the list may contain null elements. Kotlin's null-safety feature thus extends to collections interoperating with Java, requiring developers to handle potential null values explicitly, enhancing robustness and reducing the likelihood of NullPointerExceptions.

In summary, leveraging Java collections in Kotlin involves understanding and respecting the differences in how both languages handle collections, especially regarding mutability and nullability. By adhering to Kotlin's conventions and utilizing its interoperability features judiciously, developers can harness the strengths of both Java and Kotlin collections within their applications, achieving both performance and safety.

8.6 Java Generics and Kotlin Type Parameters

Understanding the correspondence between Java generics and Kotlin type parameters is pivotal for effectively leveraging interoperability between the two languages. Both Java generics and Kotlin type parameters are mechanisms that allow for the definition of classes, interfaces, and methods with type parameters, which can be specified when an instance is created or when a method is called. However, important differences in their implementations can affect interoperability.

In Java, generics are implemented using type erasure, which means

215

that generic type information is not available at runtime. This design choice was made for backward compatibility when generics were introduced in Java 5. In contrast, Kotlin's type system is designed to provide more rigorous type checks at compile-time, and it does not use type erasure in the same manner as Java. This discrepancy necessitates understanding how to work with Java generics from Kotlin and vice versa without introducing runtime errors or compromising type safety.

Calling Java Code with Generics from Kotlin

When calling Java code that uses generics from Kotlin, the Kotlin compiler tends to infer the type parameters automatically. However, in some cases, especially when dealing with raw types or complex generic structures, explicit type annotations may be required in Kotlin to ensure type safety.

Consider a Java method with the following signature:

```
1   public <T> List<T> filter(List<T> list, Predicate<T> predicate);
```

When calling this method from Kotlin, type inference simplifies the invocation, as shown below:

```
1   val filteredList = filter(listOf(1, 2, 3)) { it > 2 }
```

In this scenario, Kotlin correctly infers the generic types involved. However, care must be taken with nullability when dealing with Java generics, as Java's type system does not differentiate between nullable and non-nullable types.

Using Kotlin Type Parameters in Java

Invoking Kotlin functions with type parameters from Java is straightforward, thanks to Kotlin's interoperability features. Kotlin's type parameters are compiled in a way that makes them usable from Java code, although type erasure still applies. To preserve type information that may be needed at runtime, Kotlin offers the @JvmInline an-

216

notation for value classes and the @JvmWildcard annotation for controlling variance in type projections.

Consider a Kotlin function with the following signature:

```
1  fun <T> List<T>.customFilter(predicate: (T) -> Boolean): List<T>
```

From Java, this function can be invoked as follows:

```
1  List<Integer> myList = Arrays.asList(1, 2, 3, 4);
2  List<Integer> filteredList = CustomFilterKt.customFilter(myList, it ->
       it > 2);
```

Here, CustomFilterKt refers to the Kotlin-generated class name where the customFilter extension function is statically available. Java's lambda expressions work seamlessly with Kotlin's functional parameters, thanks to Kotlin's SAM (Single Abstract Method) conversion.

Best Practices and Considerations

- Be mindful of Kotlin's null safety when interacting with Java generics, as Java's type system does not distinguish between nullable and non-nullable types.

- Use the @JvmInline annotation in Kotlin to preserve type information for value classes when interoperating with Java.

- Employ the @JvmWildcard annotation in Kotlin to fine-tune the variance of type projections, ensuring compatibility with Java's use of wildcards.

- Explicitly specify type arguments in Kotlin when calling Java methods with complex generic structures to aid the Kotlin compiler's type inference.

While Java generics and Kotlin type parameters serve similar purposes, differences in their implementations and the handling of nullability and type erasure necessitate careful consideration when intermixing Java and Kotlin code. Adhering to the best practices outlined ensures robust interoperability and type safety across both languages.

8.7   Interoperable   Naming: @JvmName Annotation

In the continuum of Kotlin-Java interoperability, a pivotal feature is the @JvmName annotation. This annotation serves a unique purpose: it influences the naming of Kotlin elements when they are called from Java code, thereby providing flexibility and avoiding naming conflicts that can arise due to differences in naming conventions between the two languages.

Let's delve into the mechanics of the @JvmName annotation. When Kotlin compiles to Java bytecode, it often employs naming schemes that are not customary or may clash with Java's naming conventions. The @JvmName annotation provides a way to explicitly specify the name that should be used in the generated Java bytecode.

Consider the following Kotlin function:

```
1   fun List<String>.getJoinedString(separator: String): String = this.
        joinToString(separator)
```

By default, the name of the generated Java method for this function might not be intuitive for Java developers, or it might inadvertently clash with an existing Java method name. To address this, we apply the @JvmName annotation:

```
1   @JvmName("joinStringsWithSeparator")
2   fun List<String>.getJoinedString(separator: String): String = this.
        joinToString(separator)
```

In the compiled Java bytecode, the method will now have the name "joinStringsWithSeparator", making it more recognisable and eradicating potential conflicts.

The scope of @JvmName is not limited to functions. It can also be applied to file-level functions and property getters/setters, thereby broadening its applicability and utility in making Kotlin code more Java-friendly. For instance, applying @JvmName to a Kotlin property's getter method:

```
1   var _table: Map<String, Int>? = null
2
3   @get:JvmName("getTable")
4   val table: Map<String, Int>
5       get() {
6           if (_table == null) {
7               _table = HashMap() // Initialize it if it's null
8           }
9           return _table ?: throw AssertionError("Set to null by another
                thread")
10      }
```

In this code snippet, the getter for the table property will appear as getTable in the Java bytecode, adhering to Java's bean convention.

It is vital to acknowledge the constraints associated with the @JvmName annotation. It cannot be used to resolve overloads in Kotlin that would result in a signature clash in Java, nor can it be used to change the name of constructors or class names in the generated bytecode.

The @JvmName annotation is a powerful tool for managing the interoperability of names between Kotlin and Java. By enabling developers to specify alternate names for Kotlin elements in the Java bytecode, it enhances the compatibility and ease of use of Kotlin code within Java projects. As always, it is recommended to use this feature judiciously, employing it when it truly adds value and clarity to the interoperable codebase.

8.8 Creating Kotlin Extensions for Java Classes

Kotlin extension functions provide a powerful mechanism to add functionality to existing classes without inheriting from them. This feature is especially useful when working with Java classes in Kotlin code, allowing developers to enhance Java classes with Kotlin's concise and expressive syntax. In this section, the focus will be on the process of creating extension functions and properties for Java classes, illustrating how Kotlin's interoperability with Java can be leveraged to write more readable and idiomatic Kotlin code.

The first step in creating an extension function for a Java class is to declare a function with a receiver type corresponding to the Java class intended for extension. This receiver type is specified before the function name, separated by a period. The following is an example where an extension function named 'isEmptyOrNull' is created for the Java class 'String'.

```
1   fun String?.isEmptyOrNull(): Boolean = this == null || this.isEmpty()
```

In the above example, 'String¿ is the receiver type, indicating that the extension function can be called on a variable of type 'String' or on a null reference. Inside the function, 'this' refers to the instance of 'String' on which the function is invoked. The function checks if the string is 'null' or empty, showcasing how Kotlin's null safety features can be integrated seamlessly with Java classes.

Similarly, Kotlin allows the definition of extension properties for Java classes. An extension property can add a new property to a class without altering its definition. Here is an example of adding a 'reversedLength' extension property to the 'String' class.

```
1   val String.reversedLength: Int
2       get() = this.reversed().length
```

This property returns the length of the reversed string. It uses Kotlin's property syntax, combined with the 'reversed' function available on 'String' objects, to compute the length of the reversed string. The property can be accessed on any 'String' instance as if it were a member of the 'String' class.

Extension functions and properties respect Java's visibility modifiers. If a Java class or its members are declared 'private' or package-private, they cannot be accessed by Kotlin extensions directly. To work around this limitation, one can utilize Java reflection or create a public method in Java that exposes the required functionality.

Let's consider a practical scenario where extension functions and properties simplify interoperability. Assume there is a Java class 'Order' with a method 'getTotalPrice()' that returns the total price of an order as a 'BigDecimal'. In Kotlin, one might want to format this price for display. An extension function can be created for this purpose:

```
fun Order.formattedPrice(): String =
    java.text.NumberFormat.getCurrencyInstance().format(this.
        getTotalPrice())
```

This function calls 'getTotalPrice()' on the 'Order' instance (denoted by 'this'), formats it as a currency string, and returns the formatted string. The Kotlin extension directly utilizes Java's 'NumberFormat' class, illustrating the seamless interoperability between Kotlin and Java.

Extension functions and properties significantly enhance the ability of developers to write more concise and expressive Kotlin code when working with Java classes. By understanding how to extend Java classes with Kotlin, developers can utilize the best features of both languages, enabling more readable, maintainable, and idiomatic code in their applications.

8.9 Working with Kotlin and Java Annotations

Annotations are metadata tags that provide information about the code but are not part of the code itself. Annotations have become a staple in modern programming languages, including Java and Kotlin, for various purposes such as providing compiler instructions, code analysis hints, and runtime processing information. Kotlin's interoperability with Java extends to annotations, allowing developers to apply Java annotations in Kotlin code and vice versa. This section will explore how annotations function in an interoperable context between Kotlin and Java.

Applying Java Annotations in Kotlin

When working with Kotlin code that interacts with Java frameworks or libraries, you may need to use Java annotations to adhere to specific API contracts or behavior. Kotlin allows you to apply Java annotations to your Kotlin code seamlessly.

Consider the example of using the @NonNull annotation from the Java javax.annotation package to denote that a parameter in a Kotlin function cannot be null:

```
1  import javax.annotation.Nonnull
2
3  fun exampleFunction(@Nonnull param: String) {
4      println(param)
5  }
```

This usage is straightforward; the @Nonnull annotation directly precedes the parameter declaration, influencing how the Java code interoperates with this Kotlin function. When this Kotlin code is called from Java, the @Nonnull annotation enforces that the argument passed to param must not be null, integrating null safety from Kotlin into Java.

Using Kotlin Annotations in Java

Kotlin also introduces its own set of annotations that can be useful when calling Kotlin code from Java. For example, the @JvmStatic, @JvmOverloads, and @JvmField annotations control how Kotlin properties and functions are visible to Java code, allowing for more flexible interoperability.

An instance of using @JvmStatic in a Kotlin companion object, to make the annotated function or property into a static member when accessed from Java, is shown below:

```
1  class KotlinClass {
```

```
2      companion object {
3          @JvmStatic
4          fun sayHello() {
5              println("Hello from Kotlin!")
6          }
7      }
8  }
```

When the above Kotlin code is accessed from Java, the sayHello function can be called as a static method of the KotlinClass, offering a natural and idiomatic usage pattern from the perspective of Java code:

```
1  KotlinClass.sayHello(); // Calls the Kotlin companion object's method
       as static
```

Interoperating Nullability Annotations

Nullability is a prominent feature of Kotlin, designed to avoid Null-PointerExceptions. However, Java does not have this feature built into its type system. Kotlin provides nullability annotations such as @Nullable and @NonNull in its runtime, which can be helpful when Kotlin code is calling into Java, and vice versa.

When a Kotlin file declares a parameter or return type as nullable, and this code is called from Java, Kotlin's nullability annotations ensure that the Java compiler is aware of the nullability contract:

```
1  // Kotlin code
2  fun nullableReturn(): String? = null
3
4  // Java code calling the above Kotlin function
5  String result = KotlinClass.nullableReturn();
```

Kotlin's String? type is reflected into Java as annotated with @Nullable, signaling to the Java developer that the result could be null, and null checks are necessary to avoid NullPointerException.

Annotations play a critical role in Kotlin-Java interoperability, facilitating seamless integration between the two languages. By understanding how to apply and leverage annotations across Kotlin and Java, developers can ensure that their mixed-language applications are robust, consistent, and adhere to best practices around null safety, method visibility, and API contracts. Whether you are calling Java from Kotlin or Kotlin from Java, annotations provide the essential glue for fine-tuning the interaction between these two powerful languages.

8.10   Interoperability Best Practices

Ensuring a smooth interoperation between Kotlin and Java is paramount for developing robust applications that leverage the best features of both languages. This section provides a set of best practices designed to enhance interoperability, maintain code readability, and prevent common issues that may arise from the integration of Kotlin and Java.

- **Leverage the @JvmOverloads Annotation:** Kotlin functions allow default parameters, a feature not present in Java. To make these Kotlin functions more accessible from Java code, it is advisable to annotate Kotlin functions with `@JvmOverloads`. This annotation instructs the Kotlin compiler to generate overloads for this function, covering every possible combination of parameters.

  Example:

```
class ExampleClass {
    @JvmOverloads
    fun exampleFunction(param1: Int, param2: String = "
        defaultValue") {
        // Function body
    }
}
```

  Java code can then call `exampleFunction` with either one or two arguments, improving interoperability by making Kotlin's default arguments accessible from Java.

- **Explicitly Handle Nullability when Calling Java from Kotlin:** When calling Java code from Kotlin, it's important to explicitly handle nullability. Kotlin's type system distinguishes between nullable and null-safe types, whereas Java does not. When consuming Java from Kotlin, treat every Java type as nullable and perform the necessary null checks or safe calls (?) to prevent NullPointerException.

Example:

```
1  val javaObject: JavaClass = getJavaObject()
2
3  // Safe call
4  javaObject?.javaMethod()
```

- **Use Platform Types Appropriately:** Kotlin introduces the concept of platform types, denoted as T!, which comes from Java declarations and can be either null or non-null. Use Kotlin's null safety features, like the ?., ?:, and !! operators, to deal with these uncertainties properly.

- **Prefer Kotlin's Collections when Working with Java:** When dealing with collections interoperable between Kotlin and Java, prefer using Kotlin's collections as they offer more features, like a rich set of extension functions. When these collections are passed to Java, they are seamlessly converted to Java's collection types.

```
1  val kotlinList: List<String> = listOf("Item1", "Item2")
2
3  // Automatically treated as java.util.List in Java
```

- **Maintain Consistency with @JvmField, @JvmStatic, and @JvmName:** Use @JvmField for properties that need to be accessed as fields in Java, @JvmStatic in companion objects to make them accessible as static methods/fields in Java, and @JvmName to resolve naming conflicts between Kotlin and Java or to expose a different method name to Java consumers.

- **Utilize the @JvmSuppressWildcards Annotation to Deal with Generics:** When Kotlin interfaces with Java generics, wildcard types can lead to complications. To suppress wildcards generated by Kotlin, annotate the relevant type use with @JvmSuppressWildcards. This makes the integration smoother, especially when Kotlin collections are involved.

Example:

```
1   fun registerListeners(listener: List<@JvmSuppressWildcards
        EventListener>) {
2       // code to register listeners
3   }
```

- **Consider Using @file:JvmName on Kotlin Files:** To avoid classname clashes or to provide a more clear name to a Kotlin file containing top-level functions and properties, use the @file:JvmName annotation. This will give the resulting Java class a specified name, aiding in the clarity and discoverability of Kotlin-generated Java classes.

```
1   @file:JvmName("UtilityFunctions")
2   package com.example.utilities
3
4   fun utilityMethod() {}
```

Adhering to these best practices will significantly enhance the interoperability between Kotlin and Java, ensuring that codebases leveraging both languages are more maintainable, understandable, and robust.

8.11   Practical Examples of Kotlin-Java Interoperation

Let's start with a straightforward example of calling Java code from Kotlin. Suppose we have a Java class named UserManager that manages user information. This class includes a method getUserCount() which returns the total number of users.

```
1   public class UserManager {
2       private int userCount = 10; // Just for demonstration
3
4       public int getUserCount() {
```

```
5        return userCount;
6     }
7 }
```

In Kotlin, calling this Java method is as simple as calling a Kotlin method due to Kotlin's interoperability features. Here's how you would do it:

```
1 fun main() {
2     val userManager = UserManager()
3     println("User count: ${userManager.userCount}")
4 }
```

This example illustrates how seamlessly Kotlin interacts with Java. Notice that the Kotlin code directly accesses the getUserCount method of the UserManager Java class without any special syntax.

Next, we proceed to calling Kotlin code from Java. Consider a Kotlin object named OrderProcessor with a method processOrder that takes an order ID as a parameter and prints a confirmation message.

```
1 object OrderProcessor {
2     fun processOrder(orderId: String) {
3         println("Processing order: $orderId")
4     }
5 }
```

To call this Kotlin object from Java, use the following approach:

```
1 public class Main {
2     public static void main(String[] args) {
3         OrderProcessor.INSTANCE.processOrder("1234");
4     }
5 }
```

The Kotlin object is accessed with the INSTANCE field in Java, which is a singleton instance autogenerated by the Kotlin compiler.

Handling nullability in interoperable scenarios is another important aspect. Kotlin enforces null safety, whereas Java allows for null references. Suppose we have the following Kotlin function that accepts a nullable string:

227

```
1  fun printMessage(message: String?) {
2      println(message ?: "No message")
3  }
```

When calling this function from Java, it becomes crucial to handle the potential for null values to avoid unintended behavior or exceptions.

```
1  public class MessagePrinter {
2      public static void main(String[] args) {
3          String message = null;
4          KtInteropKt.printMessage(message); // Explicitly handle null
5      }
6  }
```

The Java code demonstrates cautious handling of nullability when interfacing with Kotlin code that expects nullable types.

Utilizing Java collections in Kotlin is similarly straightforward. When working with a Java method that returns a List<String>, Kotlin treats it as if it were returning a List<String?>, thus anticipating possible null elements within the collection.

```
1  fun printJavaList(javaList: List<String?>) {
2      javaList.forEach { println(it) }
3  }
```

This example shows Kotlin's accommodative stance towards Java collections, acknowledging the possible presence of null elements by default and thus preventing common errors associated with nullability.

As a final point, consider the interoperable use of generics. Suppose we have the following Java method that accepts a List of Integer and returns a List of String:

```
1  public class GenericsConverter {
2      public List<String> convertIntegersToStrings(List<Integer> numbers)
           {
3          return numbers.stream()
4                  .map(Object::toString)
5                  .collect(Collectors.toList());
6      }
7  }
```

When calling this from Kotlin, generics are seamlessly integrated:

```
1  fun main() {
2      val numbers = listOf(1, 2, 3)
3      val stringList = GenericsConverter().convertIntegersToStrings(
           numbers)
4      println(stringList)
5  }
```

The Kotlin code exhibits generics interoperability, directly utilizing the Java method without any need for adjustments regarding type parameters.

By examining these practical examples, it becomes clear how Kotlin and Java coexist and complement each other. This interoperability not only makes Kotlin a valuable addition to the Java ecosystem but also simplifies the development process, allowing developers to integrate modern Kotlin code into existing Java projects with minimal friction.

8.12 Common Pitfalls and How to Avoid Them

In this section, we focus on frequent mistakes developers encounter when working with Kotlin and Java together. By understanding these pitfalls and applying recommended strategies, developers can avoid common sources of errors and inefficiencies.

- **Ignoring Null Safety**
  One of the fundamental differences between Kotlin and Java is how they handle nullability. Kotlin's type system distinguishes between nullable and non-nullable types, whereas every reference in Java can point to null. A common mistake is neglecting to handle potential null references when calling Java code from Kotlin, leading to NullPointerExceptions.
  Solution: Always check for nullability when working with Java objects in Kotlin. You can use Kotlin's safe call operator

(?.) and the Elvis operator (?:) to deal with null references elegantly.

```
1  val javaObject: JavaClass? = JavaClass()
2  val result = javaObject?.javaMethod() ?: "Default"
```

- **Improper Use of Java Collections**
  Java collections are mutable by default, whereas Kotlin distinguishes between mutable and immutable collections. Directly using Java collections in Kotlin without considering mutability can lead to unexpected behavior.
  Solution: When you receive a collection from Java code, convert it into a Kotlin collection using the toList(), toSet(), or toMap() extension functions. For mutable collections, use toMutableList(), toMutableSet(), or toMutableMap().

```
1  val javaList: java.util.List<String> = JavaClass.getJavaList()
2  val kotlinList: List<String> = javaList.toList()
```

- **Misusing Generics**
  Java generics are erased at runtime, while Kotlin's inline reified types allow for type checks and casts that are erased in Java. Misunderstanding these differences can lead to incorrect code when interoperating.
  Solution: Be cautious with generic code that involves type checks or casts.   Use the @JvmWildcard annotation for interoperability of generic types and consider inline functions with reified type parameters in Kotlin for type-safe operations.

```
1  // Kotlin inline function with reified type
2  inline fun <reified T> List<*>.filterIsInstance(): List<T> {
3      return this.filter { it is T }.map { it as T }
4  }
```

- **Annotation Misinterpretation**
  Annotations are utilized differently in Java and Kotlin. A common pitfall is misapplying Java annotations in Kotlin code, or vice versa, especially for annotations that influence runtime behavior or serialization.
  Solution: Thoroughly   understand   the   implications   of

annotations in each language. Use Kotlin-specific annotations like @JvmStatic, @JvmOverloads, and @JvmField to control how Kotlin properties and functions are exposed to Java.

- **Platform Types Ambiguity**
  When calling Java code from Kotlin, the Kotlin compiler treats all Java types as platform types, whose nullability is unknown. Assuming non-nullability without proper checks can lead to runtime exceptions.
  Solution: Treat any type coming from Java as nullable and perform explicit null checks or use Kotlin's null-safety features to deal with potential null values.

```
1  // Example of handling a platform type
2  val javaString: String? = JavaClass.getNullableString()
3  val kotlinString = javaString ?: "default"
```

By acknowledging and addressing these common pitfalls, developers can enhance the interoperability between Kotlin and Java, leading to more robust and error-free applications.

231

Chapter 9

Data Management with Kotlin

This chapter delves into the realm of data management using Kotlin, focusing on how to handle, persist, and manipulate data effectively in Kotlin applications. It explores various strategies and tools for working with JSON and XML, interacting with databases using SQLite and the Room library, and leveraging cloud solutions like Firebase for online data management. Additionally, the chapter covers best practices for implementing data caching, managing files and directories, and utilizing Kotlin for data serialization and deserialization techniques. Through these discussions, readers will acquire the skills necessary to manage data efficiently in their Kotlin applications, ensuring robustness, scalability, and performance.

9.1 Introduction to Data Management in Kotlin

Let's start by examining the fundamental principles of data management in Kotlin. Kotlin, as a statically typed programming language, offers a variety of features that simplify the process of handling, persisting, and manipulating data. These features are conducive to building applications that are both robust and efficient. The language's design prioritizes safety, clarity, and tool support, making it an excellent choice for data management tasks.

Data management in Kotlin can be broadly categorized into handling in-memory data and persistent data. In-memory data management involves operations on data that reside temporarily in the RAM, and is lost when the application is closed or the device is restarted. Persistent data management, on the other hand, involves operations on data that is stored on a permanent storage medium, such as a disk, and remains available across sessions and reboots.

- In-memory data management typically includes defining data structures, manipulating collections, and leveraging powerful functional programming constructs offered by Kotlin.

- Persistent data management encompasses interactions with file systems, databases, and remote servers, ensuring data is stored and retrieved efficiently and securely.

Effective data management in Kotlin also necessitates an understanding of serialization and deserialization concepts. Serialization is the process of converting an object into a format that can be easily stored or transmitted (e.g., JSON, XML). Deserialization is the reverse process, where the stored or transmitted data is reconstructed back into an object. Kotlin provides comprehensive support for both these processes, enabling seamless transitions between in-memory objects and their persistent or transmitted representations.

Another crucial aspect of data management in Kotlin is error handling. Properly dealing with potential errors during data operations is essential for maintaining the integrity and reliability of the application. Kotlin introduces several mechanisms to handle errors in a controlled and expressive manner, including the use of nullable types, exceptions, and the `Result` type.

Effective data management strategies are vital for developing applications that are not only functional but also performant and scalable. As we delve deeper into each topic in this chapter, we will explore specific techniques and tools that Kotlin developers can use to manage data efficiently, including working with popular data formats like JSON and XML, interacting with SQLite and Room databases, leveraging Firebase for cloud-based data storage, and implementing caching strategies to enhance performance.

In the following segments, we will discuss the intricacies of working with JSON in Kotlin, starting with the basics of JSON parsing, moving towards more advanced topics like custom serializers and deserializers, and exploring best practices for handling JSON data effectively in Kotlin applications.

9.2   Working with JSON in Kotlin

Working with JSON (JavaScript Object Notation) in Kotlin is essential for modern applications, especially those requiring data interchange between a server and a client. JSON is a lightweight data format that is easy for humans to read and write, and easy for machines to parse and generate. Kotlin, with its concise syntax and interoperability with Java, offers a powerful environment to work with JSON.

In Kotlin, there are multiple libraries available to parse and generate JSON data. One of the most popular libraries is Gson, developed by Google. Another widely used library is Klaxon. Both libraries have their own set of APIs and ways to handle JSON data efficiently. This section will focus on using these libraries for JSON operations in Kotlin.

Using Gson in Kotlin

Gson is a Java library that can be used in Kotlin for converting Java Objects into their JSON representation and vice versa. It can work with arbitrary Java objects, including pre-existing objects that you do not have source-code of.

To use Gson in a Kotlin project, first, add the Gson library
dependency to your build.gradle file:

```
1  dependencies {
2      implementation 'com.google.code.gson:gson:2.8.6'
3  }
```

After the dependency is added, you can start using Gson to serialize and deserialize JSON. For serialization, you can convert a Kotlin
object into a JSON string as follows:

```
1  import com.google.gson.Gson
2
3  data class User(val name: String, val age: Int)
4
5  fun main() {
6      val user = User("John Doe", 30)
7      val gson = Gson()
8      val jsonString = gson.toJson(user)
9      println(jsonString)
10 }
```

This code will output a JSON string like below:

```
{"name":"John Doe","age":30}
```

For deserialization, converting a JSON string back to a Kotlin object
is straightforward:

```
1  val jsonString = '{"name":"John Doe","age":30}'
2  val user = gson.fromJson(jsonString, User::class.java)
3  println(user)
```

Using Klaxon in Kotlin

Klaxon is a lightweight library to parse JSON in Kotlin. It supports
converting JSON strings into Kotlin objects, JSON arrays into lists,
and more.

To include Klaxon in your project, add the following dependency to
your build.gradle file:

```
1  dependencies {
2      implementation 'com.beust:klaxon:5.0.1'
3  }
```

With Klaxon, you can parse a JSON string into a Kotlin object as shown below:

```
1  import com.beust.klaxon.Klaxon
2
3  data class Person(val name: String, val age: Int)
4
5  val json = """
6      {
7          "name": "Jane Doe",
8          "age": 28
9      }
10 """.trimIndent()
11
12 val person = Klaxon().parse<Person>(json)
13 println(person)
```

This will output the `Person` object constructed from the JSON string.

Handling Complex JSON Structures

When dealing with more complex JSON structures, such as nested objects or arrays, both Gson and Klaxon offer ways to handle them. For example, to parse a list of users from a JSON array with Gson, you could do:

```
1  val jsonArray = '[{"name":"John Doe","age":30},{"name":"Jane Roe","age":25}]'
2  val type = object : TypeToken<List<User>>() {}.type
3  val users = gson.fromJson<List<User>>(jsonArray, type)
4  users.forEach { println(it) }
```

Handling similar structures with Klaxon involves using the `parseArray` method:

```
1  val json = """
2      [
3          {"name": "John Doe", "age": 30},
4          {"name": "Jane Roe", "age": 25}
```

```
5      ]
6   """.trimIndent()
7
8   val people = Klaxon().parseArray<Person>(json)
9   people?.forEach { println(it) }
```

Both approaches enable the processing of complex JSON structures, facilitating the development of robust Kotlin applications that interact with JSON data.

Kotlin provides excellent support for working with JSON, a critical requirement for modern application development. Whether you choose Gson, Klaxon, or another library, Kotlin's interoperability and concise syntax make the process of serializing and deserializing JSON data straightforward and efficient.

9.3   Handling XML Data

Handling XML data efficiently is crucial for Kotlin applications that interact with XML-based APIs or require the processing of XML files. Kotlin, being a versatile programming language, offers various approaches to parsing and generating XML data. In this section, we will discuss the tools and techniques available in Kotlin for working with XML, including using standard library functions and leveraging third-party libraries like Simple XML Serialization.

Parsing XML Data in Kotlin

Parsing XML data involves reading the XML file and extracting useful information from it. Kotlin provides support for parsing XML data through its standard library, particularly with the use of the Java API for XML Processing (JAXP). However, for a more Kotlin-centric approach, third-party libraries such as Simple XML Serialization can be employed for more idiomatic Kotlin code.

Using JAXP

The Java API for XML Processing (JAXP) allows for the processing of XML data in a platform-independent manner. While it is a Java-based solution, it can be seamlessly integrated into Kotlin projects. The following example demonstrates how to use JAXP in Kotlin to parse a simple XML file:

```
import javax.xml.parsers.DocumentBuilderFactory

fun parseXML(file: File) {
    val documentBuilder = DocumentBuilderFactory.newInstance().
        newDocumentBuilder()
    val document = documentBuilder.parse(file)
    val rootElement = document.documentElement
    println("Root element: ${rootElement.nodeName}")

    if (rootElement.hasChildNodes()) {
        val children = rootElement.childNodes
        for (i in 0 until children.length) {
            val node = children.item(i)
            if (node.nodeType == Node.ELEMENT_NODE) {
                val element = node as Element
                println("Element: ${element.nodeName}, Value: ${element.
                    textContent}")
            }
        }
    }
}
```

This example demonstrates the basics of parsing an XML file, extracting the root element, and iterating over its child nodes to print the element names and their text content.

Leveraging Simple XML Serialization

For a more Kotlin-friendly approach, Simple XML Serialization offers a declarative framework for serializing and deserializing XML. This library simplifies XML handling by allowing you to annotate Kotlin classes to define how they map to XML structures. Here is how you can use Simple XML Serialization:

```
import org.simpleframework.xml.Element
```

```kotlin
import org.simpleframework.xml.Root
import org.simpleframework.xml.core.Persister

@Root(name = "employee")
data class Employee(
    @field:Element(name = "id")
    var id: Int,
    @field:Element(name = "name")
    var name: String
)

fun main() {
    val xml = """
        <employee>
            <id>123</id>
            <name>John Doe</name>
        </employee>
    """.trimIndent()

    val serializer = Persister()
    val employee = serializer.read(Employee::class.java, xml)

    println("ID: ${employee.id}, Name: ${employee.name}")
}
```

This code snippet showcases how Simple XML Serialization enables the mapping of Kotlin data classes to XML structures through annotations, making XML data handling more concise and readable.

Generating XML Data in Kotlin

Generating XML data from Kotlin objects is the reverse process of parsing. Both JAXP and Simple XML Serialization can be used for this purpose as well. To generate XML using Simple XML Serialization, you can use the writemethod of the Persister class, as shown in the parsing example above.

Handling XML data in Kotlin, whether through parsing or generation, can be accomplished using the core Java libraries or more modern, Kotlin-specific libraries like Simple XML Serialization. The choice of tooling depends on the specific requirements of your project and your preference for Java interoperability or Kotlin idiomatic expressions.

9.4   Using SQLite for Local Data Storage

Local data storage is imperative for numerous applications that require data persistence without the constant need for an internet connection. SQLite, a lightweight database, provides a convenient way for storing, accessing, and managing local data in Kotlin applications. This section will elucidate the process of integrating SQLite into Kotlin projects, creating and manipulating databases, and best practices for efficient data management.

SQLite interacts seamlessly with Kotlin through the Android SQLiteOpenHelper class, which simplifies database creation and version management. The first step towards utilizing SQLite is the instantiation of this class. Inherit SQLiteOpenHelper and override its onCreate and onUpgrade methods to manage your database structure:

```
1   class DBHelper(context: Context): SQLiteOpenHelper(context,
        DATABASE_NAME, null, DATABASE_VERSION) {
2       companion object {
3           private const val DATABASE_VERSION = 1
4           private const val DATABASE_NAME = "sample.db"
5           const val TABLE_NAME = "People"
6       }
7
8       override fun onCreate(db: SQLiteDatabase?) {
9           val CREATE_TABLE_QUERY = "CREATE TABLE $TABLE_NAME (ID INTEGER
                PRIMARY KEY, name TEXT, age INTEGER)"
10          db?.execSQL(CREATE_TABLE_QUERY)
11      }
12
13      override fun onUpgrade(db: SQLiteDatabase?, oldVersion: Int,
            newVersion: Int) {
14          db?.execSQL("DROP TABLE IF EXISTS $TABLE_NAME")
15          onCreate(db)
16      }
17  }
```

This code snippet showcases the initiation of an SQLite database with a single table named People, comprising three fields: ID, name, and

age. The onCreate method defines the SQL query for creating this
table, which is executed when the application runs for the first time
or after a re-installation. The onUpgrade method facilitates database
schema updates without losing data by dropping the existing table
and creating a new one if the database version changes.

Inserting data into the SQLite database involves preparing Content-
Values and passing them to the insert method:

```
1  fun addPerson(name: String, age: Int) {
2      val values = ContentValues()
3      values.put("name", name)
4      values.put("age", age)
5
6      val db = this.writableDatabase
7      db.insert(TABLE_NAME, null, values)
8      db.close()
9  }
```

Querying data from the SQLite database requires specifying the
columns to retrieve, the selection criteria, and the query parameters.
The following function demonstrates fetching a person's records by
their name:

```
1  fun getPerson(name: String): Cursor? {
2      val db = this.readableDatabase
3      return db.query(TABLE_NAME, arrayOf("ID", "name", "age"), "name = ?
           ", arrayOf(name), null, null, null)
4  }
```

To ensure efficient data management and application performance, it
is essential to follow best practices such as closing the database connection with db.close() after completing operations and utilizing
transactions for bulk insertions or updates.

SQLite offers a robust solution for local data storage in Kotlin applications. By following the outlined steps and adhering to best practices, developers can implement an efficient and reliable local data
management system, enhancing the application's functionality and
user experience.

9.5 Exploring Room Database with Kotlin

Room is a persistence library providing an abstraction layer over SQLite to allow for more robust database access while harnessing the full power of SQLite. The integration of Room with Kotlin enhances the efficiency and scalability of database operations in Android applications. This section elucidates the primary components of Room, the establishment of a database connection, and the execution of CRUD (Create, Read, Update, and Delete) operations through concise and operation-centric Kotlin code snippets.

First, the main architectural elements of Room which include the Database, Entity, and DAO (Data Access Object) must be understood:

- **Entity:** Represents a table within the database. Kotlin classes are annotated with @Entity to signify their role.

- **DAO:** Stands for Data Access Object. It is an interface that contains methods for accessing the database. These methods are annotated with Room-specific annotations.

- **Database:** A container that holds the database holder. It is an abstract class annotated with @Database, extending RoomDatabase.

To illustrate the process of configuring a Room database in Kotlin, consider the following scenario where we aim to store and manage user information.

Define an Entity:

```
1  @Entity(tableName = "users")
2  data class User(
3      @PrimaryKey(autoGenerate = true) val id: Int,
4      @ColumnInfo(name = "first_name") val firstName: String,
5      @ColumnInfo(name = "last_name") val lastName: String,
6      @ColumnInfo(name = "email") val email: String
7  )
```

Next, create the DAO interface:

```
1   @Dao
2   interface UserDao {
3       @Insert
4       fun insertUser(user: User)
5
6       @Query("SELECT * FROM users")
7       fun getAllUsers(): List<User>
8
9       @Delete
10      fun deleteUser(user: User)
11
12      @Update
13      fun updateUser(user: User)
14  }
```

Subsequently, establish the Room Database:

```
1   @Database(entities = [User::class], version = 1)
2   abstract class AppDatabase : RoomDatabase() {
3       abstract fun userDao(): UserDao
4   }
```

For initiating a connection with the database, leverage Room's database builder within an Android context (e.g., Activity, Fragment):

```
1   val db = Room.databaseBuilder(
2       applicationContext,
3       AppDatabase::class.java, "database-name"
4   ).build()
```

With the database setup complete, performing CRUD operations becomes straightforward. For instance, to insert a user:

```
1   val user = User(0, "John", "Doe", "john.doe@example.com")
2   db.userDao().insertUser(user)
```

Retrieving all users involves just a single line of code:

```
1   val users = db.userDao().getAllUsers()
```

Updating and deleting users follow a similar pattern, emphasizing the simplicity and power offered by Room when managing data in

Kotlin applications. Room's integration facilitates not only a structured approach to data management but also ensures type-safe, compile-time checks – reducing runtime errors and improving overall code reliability.

Leveraging Room in conjunction with Kotlin equips developers with a potent toolkit for crafting efficient, reliable Android applications with complex data management needs. It underscores the importance of understanding underlying Room concepts and their practical applications to fully benefit from this architectural component's capabilities.

9.6 Kotlin and Firebase for Online Data Management

Firebase offers a comprehensive suite of tools for the online management of data, making it an ideal choice for Kotlin developers aiming to build robust, scalable apps with minimal boilerplate code and reliable backend infrastructure. This section will discuss integrating Firebase into Kotlin applications, focusing on data management aspects such as real-time databases, user authentication, and cloud storage.

Firebase Realtime Database and Firestore are popular choices for online data management, offering real-time synchronization of data across all clients. To start using Firebase in a Kotlin project, one needs to add the necessary Firebase dependencies to the project's build.gradle file. Importantly, the Firebase Android BoM (Bill of Materials) should be included to ensure compatible versions of Firebase libraries.

First, to include Firebase Realtime Database or Firestore, add the following dependencies:

```
1  implementation 'com.google.firebase:firebase-database-ktx'
2  implementation 'com.google.firebase:firebase-firestore-ktx'
```

After syncing the project with the gradle files, you can start using

Firebase's functionalities. For instance, to write data to a Firebase Realtime Database, use the following code snippet:

```
1  val databaseReference = FirebaseDatabase.getInstance().getReference("
      messages")
2  databaseReference.setValue("Hello, Firebase!")
```

This code creates a reference to a "messages" node in the database and sets its value to "Hello, Firebase!". The use of the setValue method immediately synchronizes the data across all clients listening to this node.

Retrieving data is similarly straightforward. The following example listens for changes to the "messages" node and logs the updated value:

```
1   databaseReference.addValueEventListener(object : ValueEventListener {
2       override fun onDataChange(dataSnapshot: DataSnapshot) {
3           val value = dataSnapshot.getValue(String::class.java)
4           Log.d("File", "Value is: $value")
5       }
6
7       override fun onCancelled(error: DatabaseError) {
8           Log.w("File", "Failed to read value.", error.toException())
9       }
10  })
```

Firebase's cloud storage services, powered by Google Cloud Storage, offer robust solutions for storing user-generated content such as photos, videos, and other files. Integration into a Kotlin project involves adding the storage SDK. The SDK facilitates various operations, such as uploading and downloading files. Here is an example of how to upload a file:

```
1  val storageRef = FirebaseStorage.getInstance().reference.child("images
      /myImage.jpg")
2  val uploadTask = storageRef.putBytes(dataByteArray)
3  uploadTask.addOnFailureListener {
4      // Handle unsuccessful uploads
5  }.addOnSuccessListener { taskSnapshot ->
6      // taskSnapshot.metadata contains file metadata such as size,
         content-type, etc.
7  }
```

In this snippet, `dataByteArray` represents the byte array of the image to be uploaded. The `putBytes` method uploads the data to the specified path within Firebase cloud storage, allowing for asynchronous handling of success or failure events.

Firebase Authentication, another essential service, supports authentication using emails, phone numbers, Google, Facebook, and Twitter, among others. Integrating Firebase Authentication requires adding the Firebase Auth dependency:

```
1  implementation 'com.google.firebase:firebase-auth-ktx'
```

A simple email and password authentication flow can be implemented as follows:

```
1  FirebaseAuth.getInstance().createUserWithEmailAndPassword(email,
       password)
2      .addOnCompleteListener { task ->
3          if (task.isSuccessful) {
4              Log.d("Auth", "createUserWithEmail:success")
5              val user = FirebaseAuth.getInstance().currentUser
6              // Update UI with the signed-in user's information
7          } else {
8              Log.w("Auth", "createUserWithEmail:failure", task.exception)
9              // If sign in fails, display a message to the user.
10         }
11     }
```

This example demonstrates creating a new user account with an email and password. The `addOnCompleteListener` method allows handling the result asynchronously, offering a smooth user experience.

In summary, integrating Firebase with Kotlin applications enhances data management capabilities, offering real-time data synchronization, robust cloud storage solutions, and flexible user authentication mechanisms. With straightforward setup and minimal boilerplate code, developers can focus on building the core features of their applications, confident in the reliability and scalability of their online data management system.

9.7   Implementing Data Caching Strategies

Implementing effective data caching strategies in Kotlin applications is crucial for enhancing performance and providing a smooth user experience, especially in data-intensive applications. Data caching temporarily stores copies of data so that future requests for that data can be served faster. This section discusses key considerations and strategies for implementing data caching in Kotlin.

Understanding Caching Levels

Before diving into specific Kotlin implementations, it's important to understand the different levels at which caching can be applied:

- **Application Level Caching:** Involves storing data within the application's memory space. This is the fastest form of caching but is limited by the application's memory capacity.

- **Database Level Caching:** This involves caching queries or result sets at the database level. It's useful for reducing database load and improving query response times.

- **Distributed Caching:** Used in distributed systems to share cache data across multiple servers or instances, improving scalability and data consistency.

Implementing Caching in Kotlin

When implementing caching in Kotlin, developers can leverage various libraries and techniques. For local caching, one common approach is to use a caching library such as Caffeine, which provides an in-memory cache with a high hit rate and efficient eviction policies.

```
1   val cache = Caffeine.newBuilder()
2       .maximumSize(10_000)
3       .expireAfterWrite(5, TimeUnit.MINUTES)
4       .build<String, DataObject>()
```

In the example above, a cache is created with a maximum size of 10,000 entries and an expiration time of 5 minutes. DataObjects can be stored and retrieved from the cache using their String keys.

For distributed caching in Kotlin applications, Redis is a popular choice due to its high performance and rich feature set. Kotlin applications can interact with Redis using libraries like Lettuce or Jedis.

```
1  val redisClient = RedisClient.create("redis://localhost:6379/")
2  val connection = redisClient.connect()
3  val syncCommands = connection.sync()
4  syncCommands.set("key", "value")
```

The code snippet above demonstrates the basic setup for connecting to a Redis instance and performing a simple set operation using the Lettuce library.

Caching Strategies

Choosing the right caching strategy is pivotal for maximizing the effectiveness of your cache. Common caching strategies include:

- **Least Recently Used (LRU):** Evicts the least recently used items first. Suitable for most general-purpose caching needs.

- **Time-To-Live (TTL):** Data expires after a specified duration. Ideal for data that updates frequently or has a predictable freshness requirement.

- **Write-Through & Write-Around Caching:** These strategies involve writing data to the cache and the database simultaneously (Write-Through) or writing directly to the database and optionally to the cache (Write-Around). These strategies ensure data consistency between the cache and the database.

Best Practices for Data Caching

To effectively implement data caching in Kotlin, consider the following best practices:

- Regularly analyze and monitor cache performance and hit rates to adjust size and eviction policies as necessary.

- Use asynchronous operations for cache access to prevent blocking the main thread, especially in UI applications.

- Invalidate or update the cache proactively when data changes to ensure consistency.

- Consider security implications, especially when caching sensitive information. Encrypt cached data if necessary.

Implementing effective data caching strategies in Kotlin applications involves understanding the caching levels, selecting appropriate tools and libraries, choosing the right caching strategy, and following best practices to ensure data consistency, security, and performance.

9.8   Managing Files and Directories in Kotlin

Managing files and directories is a crucial aspect of data management in Kotlin applications.   Kotlin provides a comprehensive set of tools and APIs that simplifies the process of file operations, including creation, reading, writing, deletion, and traversal of directories.

Firstly, to create a new file, the `File` class from the Kotlin standard library is utilized. This class represents a file or directory path and provides methods to perform operations on the path it represents. The creation of a new file involves calling the `createNewFile()` method on an instance of the `File` class, which returns a Boolean indicating the success or failure of the file creation operation.

```
1   import java.io.File
2
3   fun createFile() {
4       val file = File("/path/to/your/file.txt")
5       val result = file.createNewFile()
6       if (result) {
7           println("File created successfully.")
8       } else {
9           println("File already exists.")
10      }
11  }
```

To write content to a file, the `writeText` method can be used, which directly writes a String into the file, replacing any existing content.

```
1   fun writeFile() {
2       val file = File("/path/to/your/file.txt")
3       file.writeText("Hello, Kotlin!")
4   }
```

For reading from a file, the `readText` method returns the content of the file as a String.

```
1   fun readFile() {
2       val file = File("/path/to/your/file.txt")
3       val content = file.readText()
4       println(content)
5   }
```

When it comes to directories, creating a directory involves calling the `mkdir()` method, or `mkdirs()` for creating multiple nested directories at once.

```
1   fun createDirectory() {
2       val directory = File("/path/to/your/directory")
3       val result = directory.mkdir()
4       if (result) {
5           println("Directory created successfully.")
6       } else {
7           println("Failed to create directory.")
8       }
9   }
```

Traversing directories to list files and subdirectories is done using the `listFiles()` method, which returns an array of `File` objects.

```
fun listFilesInDirectory() {
    val directory = File("/path/to/your/directory")
    val files = directory.listFiles()
    files?.forEach { file ->
        println(file.name)
    }
}
```

Deleting a file or directory is straightforward with the `delete()` method. It's important to note that deleting a directory requires that the directory is empty.

```
fun deleteFile() {
    val file = File("/path/to/your/file.txt")
    val result = file.delete()
    if (result) {
        println("File deleted successfully.")
    } else {
        println("Failed to delete file.")
    }
}
```

Handling files and directories is more than just file manipulation. It also encompasses understanding file properties and metadata. For instance, to check if the path is a file or a directory, `isFile` and `isDirectory` properties can be used.

Managing files and directories effectively is a fundamental skill in Kotlin programming. By leveraging the Kotlin standard library's `File` class and its methods, developers can perform a wide range of file operations efficiently, enabling them to handle data in a robust manner.

9.9   Using Kotlin for Data Serialization and Deserialization

Data serialization refers to the process of converting an object into a format that can be easily stored or transmitted and subsequently reconstructed. Deserialization is the reverse process, where the stored or transmitted data is used to recreate the object. Kotlin, with its concise syntax and advanced features, offers a seamless way to perform these tasks, especially when working with JSON, a lightweight data interchange format.

The Importance of Serialization in Kotlin

Kotlin's type system and language features make it an ideal choice for data serialization and deserialization tasks. With the evolution of web services and mobile applications, efficient data exchange between servers and clients has become crucial. Kotlin's interoperability with the Java Virtual Machine (JVM) and JavaScript makes it a versatile option for handling data across platforms.

Kotlin Serialization Library

The Kotlin Serialization library ('kotlinx.serialization') is a Kotlin-native approach to object serialization. It requires the least amount of boilerplate and aligns with Kotlin's philosophy of being concise yet expressive. To use this library, one must include it in the project's build file.

```
1  dependencies {
2      implementation "org.jetbrains.kotlinx:kotlinx-serialization-json
           :1.4.0"
3  }
```

You then need to apply the plugin by adding the following line to your build script:

```
1  apply plugin: 'kotlinx-serialization'
```

Defining Serializable Classes

A class needs to be annotated with '@Serializable' to indicate that it can be serialized. Consider the following example where a data class

'User' is defined:

```
1  @Serializable
2  data class User(val name: String, val age: Int)
```

This declaration makes the 'User' class ready for serialization and deserialization without the need for additional boilerplate code.

Serialization to JSON

To serialize an instance of a class to JSON, the 'Json' object's 'encodeToString' method is used.   Here is how to serialize an instance of the 'User' class:

```
1  val user = User("Jane Doe", 30)
2  val jsonString = Json.encodeToString(user)
3  println(jsonString)
```

The output will be a JSON string that represents the 'User' object:

```
{"name":"Jane Doe","age":30}
```

Deserialization from JSON

Deserialization involves converting the JSON string back into an instance of the class. This is achieved by using the 'Json' object's 'decodeFromString' method:

```
1  val jsonString = """{"name":"Jane Doe","age":30}"""
2  val user = Json.decodeFromString<User>(jsonString)
3  println(user)
```

The 'decodeFromString' method correctly reconstructs the 'User' object from the JSON string.

Handling Custom Serializers

There may be cases where automatic serialization does not fit the requirements or a custom representation is needed. Kotlin Serialization allows for custom serializers. An example of defining a custom serializer for a class that represents a point in a 2D space could look as follows:

```
@Serializable(with = PointSerializer::class)
data class Point(val x: Int, val y: Int)

object PointSerializer : KSerializer<Point> {
    override val descriptor: SerialDescriptor =
        PrimitiveSerialDescriptor("Point", PrimitiveKind.STRING)

    override fun serialize(encoder: Encoder, value: Point) {
        encoder.encodeString("${value.x},${value.y}")
    }

    override fun deserialize(decoder: Decoder): Point {
        val (x, y) = decoder.decodeString().split(',').map(String::
            toInt)
        return Point(x, y)
    }
}
```

This custom serializer encodes and decodes 'Point' objects as strings in the format "x,y".

Kotlin's support for serialization and deserialization simplifies data management tasks in applications. By utilizing the 'kotlinx.serialization' library, developers can serialize objects with minimal code and adapt to more complex scenarios by defining custom serializers. This ability to seamlessly convert between objects and their serialized forms is vital for building modern applications that rely on data exchange.

9.10 Data Validation and Error Handling

Data validation and error handling are critical components in the development of robust Kotlin applications, especially when it comes to managing data. This section will dissect the intricacies of validating input data before processing or persisting it, and systematically handling errors to maintain application stability and user experience.

Data Validation

Data validation is the process of verifying if the data meets a set of predefined criteria before it's processed by the application. This is crucial in preventing invalid or malicious data from causing unintended effects in the application's workflow. Kotlin, with its robust type system and nullable types, provides a solid foundation for implementing data validation effectively.

- **Type Validation:** Ensure the data type is as expected. Kotlin's strong typing helps in this regard, but when dealing with external input, type checks might be necessary.

- **Range Validation:** For numeric data, checking that the value falls within an expected range prevents errors that could occur from extreme or unexpected values.

- **Format Validation:** When dealing with strings, especially those that represent structured data like dates or emails, verifying the format can prevent many issues down the line.

- **Nullability Checks:** Kotlin's null safety features force developers to handle nullability explicitly, which is a form of data validation in itself, ensuring that null values are dealt with intentionally.

Implementing Data Validation

Implementing data validation in Kotlin can be done through manual checks in the code, using conditional statements, or by utilizing more sophisticated validation libraries that can simplify the process. Here is a basic example of manual data validation:

```
1  fun validateUserData(name: String, age: Int): Boolean {
2      if (name.isBlank()) {
3          println("Name cannot be blank")
4          return false
5      }
6      if (age !in 1..99) {
7          println("Age must be between 1 and 99")
```

```
8        return false
9      }
10     return true
11   }
```

This approach, while straightforward, can quickly become unwieldy for more complex validation rules or larger datasets. Leveraging Kotlin's ability to extend existing types with new functions, or using validation libraries, can lead to more maintainable code.

Error Handling

When an error occurs, knowing how to handle it effectively is as important as preventing it. Kotlin offers several mechanisms for error handling, with the most common being the try-catch block.

```
1   try {
2       val result = riskyOperation()
3       println("Result: $result")
4   } catch (e: Exception) {
5       println("Error occurred: ${e.message}")
6   }
```

For more granular control, Kotlin provides the `try`, `catch`, `finally`, and use constructs, each serving a specific purpose in the error handling paradigm. The use function, in particular, is designed for handling AutoCloseable resources, automatically closing them once the operation is completed, even if an error occurs.

```
1   File("data.txt").bufferedReader().use { reader ->
2       val data = reader.readLine()
3       println(data)
4   }
```

Best Practices for Data Validation and Error Handling

When implementing data validation and error handling in Kotlin applications, adhering to best practices ensures the reliability and maintainability of the codebase:

257

- Validate data at the earliest possible point in the data flow, ide-ally at the system's boundaries.

- Use Kotlin's expressivity to write concise and readable valida-tion and error handling logic.

- Leverage Kotlin's built-in features, such as nullable types and extension functions, to enforce data integrity.

- Employ third-party libraries judiciously to avoid reinventing the wheel, especially for complex validation scenarios.

- Implement comprehensive error handling that not only logs er-rors but also provides meaningful feedback to the user or call-ing function.

Effective data validation and error handling are indispensable in crafting resilient software. Kotlin, with its modern language features, offers developers the tools to implement these practices efficiently, contributing to the robustness of the application.

9.11   Best Practices for Data Management

Effective data management forms the backbone of any robust application. It ensures that data is not just stored but is done so in a manner that guarantees integrity, efficiency, and security. Kotlin, with its modern syntax and features, offers a wide array of tools and techniques for superior data handling. This section encapsulates the essential strategies and practices for optimized data management within Kotlin applications, focusing on principles that uphold data quality, facilitate seamless data operations, and bolster application performance.

Ensure Data Integrity and Security:

Data integrity and security are paramount in any application. Adhering to these principles involves implementing measures that prevent unauthorized data access and manipulation. Kotlin applications can leverage Kotlin's null safety and immutable types to avoid unexpected null pointer exceptions and ensure that data remains unchanged once set.

```
1   val immutableList: List<String> = listOf("Alice", "Bob", "Charlie")
```

In the context of databases or online data storage, employ user authentication, data encryption, and SQL injection prevention techniques to safeguard your data. Utilize prepared statements in SQLite and parameterized queries with Room to further protect against SQL injection attacks.

Leverage Kotlin Extensions for Enhanced Data Operations:

Kotlin's extension functions provide a powerful mechanism to extend the functionality of classes without inheriting from them. You can create intuitive and concise extensions for common data manipulation operations, leading to cleaner and more maintainable code.

```
1   fun String.toTitleCase(): String {
2       return this.split(" ").joinToString(" ") { it.capitalize() }
3   }
```

This extension function can be applied on any string instance to convert it to title case, thereby enhancing readability when dealing with text data.

Adopt a Clean Architecture:

A clean architecture separates concerns and simplifies data management by organizing code into layers, each with a distinct responsibility. In Kotlin applications, leverage the Model-View-ViewModel (MVVM) pattern for this separation. This not only makes the codebase easier to navigate but also facilitates efficient data flow and manipulation across different application components.

Utilize Caching and Offline Storage:

Strategic data caching and offline storage can drastically improve your application's performance and responsiveness. Use Kotlin's delegated properties to lazily load data or cache results of expensive operations. For offline storage, SQLite and Room databases are robust options allowing data persistence on local storage, thereby

ensuring your application remains functional even without an
internet connection.

Prefer Data Serialization Libraries:

For handling complex data structures and simplifying data
serialization and deserialization, Kotlin offers support for several
libraries, like kotlinx.serialization and Gson.   These libraries
significantly reduce the boilerplate code associated with converting
data between its representation in memory and its serialized form
in JSON or XML, thus streamlining the data management process.

```
1  @Serializable
2  data class User(val name: String, val age: Int)
```

This Kotlin data class decorated with the @Serializable annotation
indicates that kotlinx.serialization should handle its serialization and
deserialization processes, simplifying data persistence and retrieval
operations.

Implement Thorough Error Handling and Validation:

Robust error handling and data validation mechanisms are essential
for sustaining data integrity and enhancing user experience.
Kotlin's exception handling features, along with its support for
working with nullable types, facilitate comprehensive error
management strategies. Moreover, utilize regular expressions and
custom validation logic to validate inputs before processing or
storing data, thereby preventing corrupt or undesired data from
entering the system.

Adhere to Principles of Scalability and Performance:

As applications grow, their data management requirements evolve.
Ensure your data management strategies are scalable by opting for
efficient data structures, optimizing database queries, and employing asynchronous operations and coroutines for resource-intensive
tasks. Kotlin's support for these features enables developers to build
applications that perform well and scale gracefully.

Successful data management in Kotlin applications hinges on
understanding and applying a combination of best practices tailored

towards data integrity, security, and performance. By leveraging Kotlin's features and adhering to these principles, developers can ensure their applications are robust, reliable, and scalable.

9.12 Exploring Third-party Libraries for Data Management

In the pursuit of effective data management in Kotlin applications, the exploration of third-party libraries is indispensable. These libraries offer extended functionalities, optimized processes, and enhanced performance for data handling tasks which might otherwise require extensive boilerplate code. This section will dissect some of the most influential third-party libraries, elucidating their features, advantages, and how they can be integrated into Kotlin projects.

Gson for JSON Manipulation

The Gson library, developed by Google, stands out for its proficiency in converting Java Objects into JSON and back. Unlike traditional JSON parsing which can be cumbersome and error-prone, Gson provides a straightforward approach.

```
1  val gson = Gson()
2  val json = gson.toJson(userObject)
3  val user: User = gson.fromJson(json, User::class.java)
```

The code snippet above illustrates the conversion of a User object into a JSON string and vice versa. The simplicity and readability of the code demonstrate Gson's ease of use.

Retrofit for Network Operations

Retrofit is a type-safe REST client for Android and Java environments, making it a perfect candidate for Kotlin applications

needing to interact with web services. It integrates seamlessly with
Kotlin's coroutines, offering an asynchronous, non-blocking
approach to network calls.

```
interface ApiService {
    @GET("users/{user}/repos")
    suspend fun listRepos(@Path("user") user: String): List<Repo>
}
```

The code snippet defines an interface for Retrofit to handle network
requests. The @GET annotation specifies the HTTP operation, making
it evident how Retrofit simplifies API interactions.

Realm as a Mobile Database

Realm is a lightweight, yet powerful database solution designed for
mobile applications. It supports complex data types, offers fast query
execution, and ensures real-time data sync.

```
val realm = Realm.getDefaultInstance()
realm.executeTransaction { realm ->
    val user = realm.createObject(User::class.java, userId)
    user.name = "John Doe"
}
```

This snippet showcases the creation and storage of a User object in
Realm. The ease of executing transactions and modifying data illustrates Realm's user-friendly approach.

ExoPlayer for Media Storage and Retrieval

While not solely a data management library, ExoPlayer offers extensive capabilities in handling media files, making it an invaluable tool
for applications requiring multimedia data management.

```
val player = SimpleExoPlayer.Builder(context).build()
player.prepare()
player.play()
```

Through a few lines of code, ExoPlayer can initialize media

playback, showcasing its simplicity and effectiveness for media-related data handling.

Moshi for Lightweight JSON Parsing

Moshi, another JSON parsing library, stands out for its lightweight nature and minimalistic approach. It focuses on reducing app footprint and processing overhead, making it ideal for applications sensitive to performance and resource consumption.

```
1  val moshi = Moshi.Builder().build()
2  val jsonAdapter = moshi.adapter(User::class.java)
3  val json = jsonAdapter.toJson(userObject)
4  val user = jsonAdapter.fromJson(jsonString)
```

The provided code demonstrates the conversion of a User object to and from JSON. Moshi's API is exceedingly straightforward, emphasizing its goal of simplicity and efficiency.

Conclusion on Third-party Libraries

The libraries discussed herein represent a fraction of the tools available for enhancing data management in Kotlin applications. Their selection should be guided by the specific needs of the project, considering factors such as the type of data, the scale of data operations, and platform-specific requirements. By integrating these libraries, developers can significantly reduce development time, ensure code maintainability, and enhance application performance and scalability.

Chapter 10

Building Android Apps with Kotlin

This chapter provides a comprehensive overview of developing Android applications using Kotlin, showcasing why Kotlin has become the preferred language for modern Android development. It walks readers through setting up the Android development environment, creating their first app, and understanding the core components of Android architecture. Key topics include designing user interfaces, handling user interactions, implementing navigation, and managing data. Additionally, the chapter covers advanced features such as adding multimedia capabilities and integrating networking libraries. By the end of this chapter, readers will be equipped with the knowledge and tools to build robust, user-friendly Android applications with Kotlin.

10.1 Getting Started with Android Development in Kotlin

Let's start with establishing Kotlin as the primary programming language for Android development. Kotlin, a statically typed programming language running on the Java Virtual Machine (JVM), is renowned for its concise syntax and interoperability with Java code, making it an optimal choice for Android development. It is officially supported by Google for mobile development on the Android platform. This section delineates the initial steps to embark on Android development using Kotlin, including setting up the Integrated Development Environment (IDE) and creating a simple Android application.

The first step in Android development using Kotlin involves installing Android Studio, the official IDE for Android development. Android Studio provides all the necessary tools for Android app development, including a code editor, debugging tools, and emulators. It is integrated with Kotlin, hence offering a seamless development experience. To download Android Studio, visit the official Android Developer website and choose the version compatible with your operating system.

Upon successful installation of Android Studio, launch the IDE and select 'Start a new Android Studio project' to create a new project. The process requires configuring several aspects such as:

- Choosing a project template: For beginners, selecting the 'Empty Activity' template is recommended as it provides a basic structure for an Android application.

- Naming the project: Give your project a name, which will be used internally within Android Studio and as the application name.

- Specifying a save location: Choose a directory to save your project.

- Selecting the language: Ensure Kotlin is selected as the

programming language for your project.

- Choosing the minimum API level: The API level determines the minimum version of Android your application can run on. It is advisable to choose an API level that covers a significant percentage of devices while not being too outdated.

After configuring the project settings, click 'Finish'. Android Studio then generates a basic project with a 'MainActivity.kt' file, which represents the main entry point of your application.

The automatically generated code in 'MainActivity.kt' should look similar to the following:

```
1   package com.example.myfirstapp
2
3   import androidx.appcompat.app.AppCompatActivity
4   import android.os.Bundle
5
6   class MainActivity : AppCompatActivity() {
7       override fun onCreate(savedInstanceState: Bundle?) {
8           super.onCreate(savedInstanceState)
9           setContentView(R.layout.activity_main)
10      }
11  }
```

This code snippet makes 'MainActivity' a subclass of 'AppCompatActivity', a base class for activities that use the support library for compatibility with different versions of Android. The 'onCreate' method is a lifecycle callback that runs when the activity is created, and 'setContentView(R.layout.activity_main)' sets the user interface layout for this activity.

The layout file 'activity_main.xml' located under 'res/layout' defines the user interface. It contains a 'TextView' widget by default that can display text to the user.

To run the application, select an Android device or an emulator and click the 'Run' button in Android Studio. This will compile the application, install it on the selected device or emulator, and launch it.

In summary, setting up the development environment for Android applications in Kotlin and creating a basic application involves installing Android Studio, configuring a new project, understanding the structure of the project files, and running the application on a device or emulator. This foundational knowledge is crucial for diving deeper into more advanced concepts in Android development.

10.2   Setting Up Your Android Development Environment

Setting up the Android development environment is a crucial first step in developing Android apps with Kotlin. This process involves installing the Android Studio Integrated Development Environment (IDE), configuring the Android Software Development Kit (SDK), and setting up a virtual device or configuring a physical device for testing.

Installing Android Studio

Android Studio is the official IDE for Android development, built on JetBrains' IntelliJ IDEA technology. Follow these steps to download and install Android Studio:

- Visit the official Android Studio download page: https://developer.android.com/studio.

- Click on the "Download Android Studio" button.

- Accept the terms and conditions and download the installer for your operating system.

- Run the downloaded installer and follow the installation wizard's instructions.

- Once installed, launch Android Studio, and follow the setup wizard, which helps install essential components including the Android SDK.

Configuring the Android SDK

The Android SDK includes the necessary tools to develop, build, and test your applications. Android Studio typically guides you through the SDK setup, but manual configuration may sometimes be necessary:

- Open Android Studio and go to `File > Settings` (on Windows) or `Android Studio > Preferences` (on macOS).

- Navigate to the `Appearance & Behavior > System Settings > Android SDK`.

- Ensure the correct SDK Platforms are installed for the target version of Android you wish to develop for. It is recommended to install the latest SDK version and any other versions your app plans to support.

- In the SDK Tools tab, ensure that tools such as the Android SDK Build-Tools, Android Emulator, and Android SDK Platform-Tools are selected and installed.

- Apply changes and the SDK Manager will download and install any selected packages.

Setting Up Virtual Devices

For testing without a physical Android device, Android Studio provides a virtual device manager (AVD Manager) where you can configure and run Android Virtual Devices (AVDs).

- To set up a new AVD, open Android Studio and navigate to `Tools > AVD Manager`.

- Click "Create Virtual Device".

- Select a device definition that best matches the hardware you wish to emulate.

- Choose a system image, for example, a version of the Android operating system. It's advisable to download a system image with Google Play Services for testing APIs.

- Configure virtual device settings and click "Finish".

Configuring Physical Devices

To test apps on a physical device, enable Developer options and USB Debugging on the device:

- Open the Settings app on your Android device.

- Go to `About phone` and tap on the Build number 7 times to enable Developer options.

- Return to the main Settings screen, then to `Developer options`, and enable USB Debugging.

- Connect the device to your computer via USB. Android Studio should detect the device and enable deployment and debugging.

Successfully setting up the Android development environment is a fundamental step that paves the way for building Android applications with Kotlin. Correct installation and configuration of Android Studio, the Android SDK, and setting up virtual or physical devices for testing are key components of this setup process. Upon completing these steps, you will be well-prepared to start creating your first Android app with Kotlin.

10.3   Creating Your First Android App with Kotlin

Let's begin the practical journey into Kotlin by creating our first Android application using this statically typed programming language.

Kotlin is designed to fully interoperate with Java, and it employs concise syntax compared to Java, making it a preferable choice for Android development. Google officially supports Kotlin for Android development, further legitimizing its use in the Android ecosystem.

The first step in creating an Android application with Kotlin is to ensure that the Android Studio IDE is installed on your computer. Android Studio provides a comprehensive set of development tools and a seamless experience for developing Android apps. It includes features like code completion, a flexible build system, and a rich layout editor. If you haven't installed Android Studio yet, you can download it from the official Android developer website.

Once Android Studio is installed and configured, follow these steps to create your first Android app:

1. Open Android Studio and select *Start a new Android Studio project* from the options available on the welcome screen.

2. On the *Choose your project* template screen, select *Empty Activity*. This template creates an application with a single empty activity which is a good starting point for our first project.

3. Click *Next* to proceed.

4. In the *Configure your project* screen, you need to provide some information about your project:

   - **Name:** Give your project a name, such as 'MyFirstKotlinApp'.

   - **Package name:** This is usually your domain name in reverse followed by the application name. For example, 'com.example.myfirstkotlinapp'.

   - **Save location:** Choose where on your computer you'd like to save the project files.

   - **Language:** Select 'Kotlin'.

   - **Minimum API level:** Choose the minimum Android version you want your app to support. Selecting a lower version increases app compatibility but may limit access to

271

newer Android features. It's generally a good balance to select API 21 (Android 5.0 Lollipop) which covers a broad range of devices while still providing access to newer Android features.

5. Click *Finish* to create your project.

Upon completion of these steps, Android Studio takes a few moments to set up your project environment. When the process completes, you are presented with the main work interface of Android Studio, showing your project structure on the left and the code editor in the center.

The project structure contains several important files and directories, of which the following are noteworthy for beginners:

- `app -> src -> main -> java`: This directory contains the Kotlin source files for your app.

- `app -> src -> main -> res`: This directory contains resources such as layout XML files, string values, and images.

- `app -> src -> main -> AndroidManifest.xml`: The manifest file describes the fundamental characteristics of the app and defines each of its components.

To run the application, click on the green 'Run' button located on the top toolbar, or press Shift + F10. Android Studio will then prompt you to select a deployment target. If you have an Android device connected, you can select it, or alternatively, you can use the Android Emulator. After selecting the deployment target, Android Studio installs the application on the chosen device, and the app launches displaying a blank screen, which signifies the successful creation of your first Kotlin-based Android application.

In the following sections, we will delve deeper into the intricacies of Android development with Kotlin, including elaborating on the Android application architecture, UI design, user interaction, and more advanced topics. "'latex

10.4 Understanding Android Architecture and Lifecycle

Understanding the architecture of Android apps and the lifecycle of their components is crucial for effective Android development in Kotlin. This section will elucidate the foundational structure of Android applications, focusing on the Activity lifecycle, the role of Fragments, and the Android app architecture best practices as recommended by Google.

Activity Lifecycle

An Activity in Android represents a single screen with a user interface. For instance, an email application might have one activity showing a list of emails, another activity to compose an email, and another to read emails. Given that activities are the entry points for interacting with the user, understanding their lifecycle is paramount.

The lifecycle of an Activity is defined by a series of callbacks that allows the activity to know that a state has changed: the system is creating, stopping, or resuming an activity, or destroying the process in which the activity resides.

- onCreate(): The system calls this callback when creating the activity. Essential initializations and all UI setups should be performed here. It is the state where the activity is not visible yet.

- onStart(): This callback makes the activity visible to the user.

- onResume(): When the activity enters this state, it comes to the foreground, and then it can interact with the user.

- onPause(): The system calls this method as the first indication that the user is leaving the activity. It indicates that the activity is no longer in the foreground.

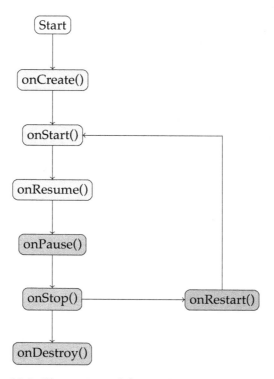

Figure 10.1: Illustration of the Android Activity Lifecycle

- onStop(): The activity is no longer visible to the user.

- onRestart(): This callback is called when the activity has stopped and is about to start again.

- onDestroy(): The system calls this before the activity is destroyed. It is the final call that the activity receives.

Fragment Lifecycle

While an Activity is designed to represent a single screen, Fragments are reusable components that can be part of multiple activities. A Fragment has its own lifecycle which is closely intertwined with its hosting activity's lifecycle.

The significant callbacks in the Fragment lifecycle include:

- onAttach(): The fragment is associated with its context.

- onCreate(): Similar to an Activity's onCreate, this is where to initialize essential components of the fragment.

- onCreateView(): This method is for creating the view hierarchy associated with the fragment.

- onActivityCreated(): Called when the activity's onCreate() method has returned.

- onStart(), onResume(), onPause(), onStop(), and onDestroy(): These have similar roles as in the lifecycle of an Activity.

- onDestroyView(): Indicates the fragment is about to be destroyed.

- onDetach(): The fragment is detached from its current activity.

Understanding both the Activity and Fragment lifecycles is pivotal for managing the user interface, data, and resources efficiently in Android apps.

Android App Architecture

Google recommends adopting the Model-View-ViewModel (MVVM) architecture for Android apps to separate the app's data from the user interface. According to MVVM, the app should be divided into three main components:

- **Model**: This represents the data and the business logic of the app. It is responsible for handling the database, network operations, or any data manipulations.

- **View**: The View is responsible for drawing data on the screen. In Android, this could be an Activity, Fragment, or any UI elements.

- **ViewModel**: It acts as a link between the Model and the View. It is responsible for transforming the data from the Model in such a way that it can be easily presented by the View.

Adhering to the MVVM architecture results in a well-structured and organized codebase that is easier to maintain and test.

This introduction to the Android architecture and lifecycle is a solid foundation for new Kotlin developers venturing into Android app development. A deep understanding of these concepts ensures the creation of efficient, maintainable, and robust Android applications.
'''

10.5   Designing User Interfaces with XML and Kotlin

Designing user interfaces (UI) in Android applications is a critical step in creating an engaging and intuitive user experience. In Android development, UI design can be accomplished through two primary methods: declaratively using XML (Extensible Markup Language) and programmatically using Kotlin. This section discusses both approaches, highlighting their strengths, use cases, and how they can be effectively utilized in tandem to build aesthetically pleasing and functional Android applications.

Understanding XML for UI Design

XML is the cornerstone of Android UI design. It provides a structured, readable format for defining UI elements and their layout properties. The use of XML allows developers to separate the application's UI design from the business logic coded in Kotlin, enhancing maintenance and scalability.

```
<TextView
    android:id="@+id/textViewHelloWorld"
    android:layout_width="wrap_content"
    android:layout_height="wrap_content"
    android:text="Hello World!"
    android:layout_centerInParent="true" />
```

In the example above, a `TextView` is defined with specific layout parameters. `android:id` provides a unique identifier for the element, whereas `android:layout_width` and `android:layout_height` define the size. The text "Hello World!" is set to be displayed at the center of its parent container using `android:layout_centerInParent`.

Leveraging Kotlin for Dynamic UIs

While XML excels at static layouts, Kotlin comes into play when creating dynamic and interactive UI components. Kotlin allows developers to manipulate UI elements programmatically, responding to user interactions or changes in application state.

```
1  val textView: TextView = findViewById(R.id.textViewHelloWorld)
2  textView.text = "Changed Text"
```

The code snippet retrieves the `TextView` defined in the XML by its ID and sets its text property to "Changed Text". This dynamic manipulation enables complex UI behaviors beyond the static declarations in XML.

Combining XML and Kotlin

Effective Android UI design often requires a synergistic approach, leveraging both XML for layout definitions and Kotlin for dynamic behaviors.

1. **Define UI structure with XML:** Start by defining the UI components and their arrangements using XML. This approach provides a clear and visual structure of the application's interface.

2. **Inflate Layouts in Kotlin:** Use Kotlin to load the XML layouts using the setContentView() method. This process, known as inflation, makes the XML-defined UI active within the application.

3. **Manipulate UI elements in Kotlin:** Access and modify the UI elements programmatically in Kotlin to handle user interactions or update UI states. This approach allows for dynamic and responsive designs.

Best Practices

- **Use meaningful IDs for UI elements in XML** to ensure that they can be easily referenced in Kotlin code.

- **Leverage the power of ConstraintLayout** for creating complex and flexible layouts with flat view hierarchies.

- **Optimize UI responsiveness** by performing heavy computations or network calls in background threads, updating the UI on the main thread.

- **Utilize data binding or view binding** to create a more direct link between the UI elements and the underlying data, minimizing boilerplate code.

Mastering UI design in Android involves understanding and effectively utilizing both XML for layout structure and Kotlin for dynamic UI manipulation. By combining these two approaches, developers can create intuitive, responsive, and visually appealing applications.

10.6   Handling User Interaction and Events

Handling user interaction is crucial for making Android applications interactive and responsive to user actions. Kotlin, with its concise syntax and interoperability with Android APIs, offers a powerful way to handle clicks, touches, and various user inputs.

Understanding Event Listeners

Event listeners in Android serve as the foundation for handling user interactions. An event listener is essentially an interface in the Android SDK that contains one or more callback methods. These methods are invoked when a user performs certain actions, such as tapping on a screen. Kotlin simplifies the process of implementing these listeners with lambda expressions and anonymous functions, resulting in cleaner and more readable code.

Implementing Click Listeners

To handle a button click in Kotlin, you first need to obtain a reference to the button in your layout. This can be done using the findViewById method or by using Kotlin Android Extensions, which allow you to reference UI components directly by their ID without the boilerplate code.

```
val button: Button = findViewById(R.id.button_example)
button.setOnClickListener {
    // Code to be executed when the button is clicked
}
```

This example demonstrates the use of a lambda expression to register an OnClickListener for a button. Within the lambda, you can define the actions to be performed when the button is clicked.

Handling Touch Events

In addition to simple clicks, Android apps may need to handle more complex touch interactions, such as swipes and multi-touch gestures. This is achieved by implementing an OnTouchListener.

```kotlin
view.setOnTouchListener { v, event ->
    when (event.action) {
        MotionEvent.ACTION_DOWN -> {
            // User started touching the screen
        }
        MotionEvent.ACTION_MOVE -> {
            // User is moving their finger on the screen
        }
        MotionEvent.ACTION_UP -> {
            // User lifted their finger off the screen
        }
    }
    true // Return true to consume the touch event
}
```

This snippet of code sets an OnTouchListener on a view and uses a when expression to determine the type of touch event (action down, move, or up) that occurred, allowing for customized responses to different touch actions.

Working with Gestures

For more sophisticated interactions, Android offers gesture detectors. The GestureDetector class allows apps to detect various gestures, such as long presses, swipes, and double taps.

```kotlin
val gestureDetector = GestureDetector(this, object : GestureDetector.
    SimpleOnGestureListener() {
    override fun onLongPress(e: MotionEvent?) {
        // Code to be executed on a long press
    }

    override fun onFling(e1: MotionEvent?, e2: MotionEvent?, velocityX:
        Float, velocityY: Float): Boolean {
        // Code to be executed on a fling gesture
        return true
    }
```

```
10  })
```

To use a `GestureDetector`, you instantiate it by passing a context and a `SimpleOnGestureListener`. The listener provides methods that you can override to handle specific gesture events.

Responding to Keyboard Inputs

Handling keyboard input is another aspect of managing user interaction. Listening for key events is important, especially for applications that require customized response to hardware keys or complex input scenarios.

```
1   view.setOnKeyListener { v, keyCode, event ->
2       if (event.action == KeyEvent.ACTION_DOWN) {
3           when (keyCode) {
4               KeyEvent.KEYCODE_ENTER -> {
5                   // Code to be executed when the Enter key is pressed
6                   true
7               }
8               else -> false
9           }
10      } else {
11          false
12      }
13  }
```

This code snippet demonstrates how to listen for key events on a view. By checking the `keyCode` in a when expression, specific actions can be executed based on which key is pressed.

In summary, Kotlin and Android provide a comprehensive framework for handling various types of user interactions, including clicks, touches, gestures, and keyboard inputs. By leveraging Kotlin's concise syntax and the Android SDK's robust set of event listeners and gesture detectors, developers can easily implement responsive and interactive UIs in their applications.

10.7   Working with Android Layouts and Material Design

Working with Android layouts and understanding Material Design principles are crucial for creating visually appealing and user-friendly applications with Kotlin. This section will explore how Kotlin interacts with XML to design layouts, harnessing Material Design to enhance user interface (UI) components and ensure an enriching user experience (UX).

In Kotlin, UI elements are typically defined using XML files within the res/layout directory of an Android project. Kotlin and XML collaborate seamlessly, allowing developers to define their app's UI structure declaratively. To manipulate these elements programmatically, Kotlin provides direct access through generated binding objects or findViewById method calls.

Let's delve into creating a simple layout using the LinearLayout, which arranges its children in a single column or row. The following XML code snippet demonstrates a vertical LinearLayout containing a TextView and a Button:

```
<LinearLayout xmlns:android="http://schemas.android.com/apk/res/
    android"
    android:layout_width="match_parent"
    android:layout_height="match_parent"
    android:orientation="vertical" >

    <TextView
        android:id="@+id/textView"
        android:layout_width="wrap_content"
        android:layout_height="wrap_content"
        android:text="Welcome to Kotlin Android Development!" />

    <Button
        android:id="@+id/button"
        android:layout_width="wrap_content"
        android:layout_height="wrap_content"
        android:text="Click Me!" />

</LinearLayout>
```

To refer to these UI components from Kotlin, the following code is utilized:

```
1  val textView: TextView = findViewById(R.id.textView)
2  val button: Button = findViewById(R.id.button)
```

Material Design, Google's design language, offers guidelines for designing UIs. It emphasizes the use of elevations, animation, and transitions to provide depth and visual feedback. Android provides Material Components to easily implement these guidelines. For example, to add a FloatingActionButton (FAB) with Material Design attributes, the following steps are followed:

First, ensure the application's build.gradle file includes the Material Components library:

```
1  dependencies {
2      implementation 'com.google.android.material:material:1.4.0'
3  }
```

Next, a FloatingActionButton can be added to a layout file:

```
1  <com.google.android.material.floatingactionbutton.FloatingActionButton
2      android:id="@+id/fab"
3      android:layout_width="wrap_content"
4      android:layout_height="wrap_content"
5      android:src="@drawable/ic_add"
6      app:layout_anchor="@id/main_content"
7      app:layout_anchorGravity="bottom|end" />
```

Integrating Material Design in an app not only embellishes the UI but also provides a standard way to achieve a polished and consistent UX across various Android devices.

Kotlin and the Android framework simplify the code needed to modify UI components, such as changing properties of a TextView dynamically:

```
1  textView.text = "Hello, Material Design!"
2  textView.setTextColor(ContextCompat.getColor(this, R.color.
       design_default_color_primary))
```

Lastly, to ensure best practices in UI/UX design, it is advised to follow the Material Design guidelines, which are regularly updated to accommodate emerging design patterns and user expectations. Embracing these principles will significantly enhance the usability and appeal of your Android applications developed with Kotlin.

10.8   Implementing   Navigation   and Multi-Screen Apps

Implementing navigation in an Android application involves managing transitions between different screens or activities. Kotlin, in conjunction with Android Jetpack's Navigation component, streamlines the process of implementing sophisticated navigation patterns, such as graphical navigation flows. This section explores the steps to set up navigation in a multi-screen Android app using Kotlin.

Firstly, integrate the Navigation component into your project. Add the necessary dependencies to your app's build.gradle file:

```
1  dependencies {
2      implementation "androidx.navigation:navigation-fragment-ktx:2.3.5"
3      implementation "androidx.navigation:navigation-ui-ktx:2.3.5"
4  }
```

After syncing the project, the next step involves creating a navigation graph. The navigation graph serves as a blueprint for the app's navigational structure, visually representing the relationships between different destinations (activities or fragments). To create a navigation graph:

1. Open the Project pane, and navigate to the res directory. 2. Right-click on the res directory, select New > Android Resource File. 3. Name the file (e.g., nav_graph), select Navigation as the Resource type, and click OK.

The Navigation Editor opens, allowing the addition of destinations to the navigation graph. Each destination corresponds to a screen in the app. To add a destination:

- Click on the New Destination button in the Navigation Editor.

- Select the fragment or activity you wish to add as a destination.

After adding destinations, relationships between them (known as actions) can be established by dragging arrows from one destination to another. These actions allow users to navigate through the app using buttons, gestures, or programmatically.

To navigate programmatically using Kotlin, retrieve an instance of NavController from a fragment or activity, and call navigate() with the ID of the action to be performed:

```
1  button.setOnClickListener {
2      findNavController().navigate(R.id.next_action)
3  }
```

Where R.id.next_action represents the action defined in the navigation graph.

Additionally, the Navigation component simplifies the implementation of Up and Back actions, ensuring consistent and predictable navigation behavior across the app. This behavior is automatically handled by the Navigation component when the app's activity extends AppCompatActivity and uses the NavigationUI class to set up the ActionBar:

```
1   override fun onCreate(savedInstanceState: Bundle?) {
2       super.onCreate(savedInstanceState)
3       setContentView(R.layout.activity_main)
4       val navController = findNavController(R.id.nav_host_fragment)
5       NavigationUI.setupActionBarWithNavController(this, navController)
6   }
7
8   override fun onSupportNavigateUp(): Boolean {
9       val navController = findNavController(R.id.nav_host_fragment)
10      return navController.navigateUp() || super.onSupportNavigateUp()
11  }
```

To implement complex navigation patterns, such as conditional navigation, nested graphs can be utilized to group related screens, making the management of large and complex navigation flows more organized and maintainable.

In summary, the Navigation component significantly simplifies the

implementation of navigation in Android apps, offering a
declarative approach to defining navigational flows. By leveraging
Kotlin and the Navigation component, developers can create
intuitive, user-friendly multi-screen applications with ease.

10.9   Data Persistence: Room, Preferences, and Files

Data persistence in Android applications is a critical aspect of app
development, enabling the storage and retrieval of user data across
app sessions. Kotlin, being Android's preferred language, works
seamlessly with various persistence mechanisms, including Room
for databases, SharedPreferences for lightweight data storage, and
file systems for direct file handling. This section will dissect these
mechanisms, elucidating their implementations and best practices
in Kotlin.

Room Database

Room provides an abstraction layer over SQLite, simplifying
database access and ensuring compile-time verification of SQL
queries. To incorporate Room into your Kotlin Android project,
begin by adding the necessary dependencies in your Gradle file:

```
dependencies {
    def room_version = "2.3.0"
    implementation "androidx.room:room-runtime:$room_version"
    annotationProcessor "androidx.room:room-compiler:$room_version"
    // For Kotlin use kapt instead of annotationProcessor
    kapt "androidx.room:room-compiler:$room_version"
}
```

Define your data entities by annotating your Kotlin data classes with
@Entity. For instance:

```
@Entity
data class User(
    @PrimaryKey val uid: Int,
    @ColumnInfo(name = "first_name") val firstName: String?,
    @ColumnInfo(name = "last_name") val lastName: String?
```

```
6  )
```

Next, create a Data Access Object (DAO) interface. This interface
serves as a contract for accessing your data:

```
1  @Dao
2  interface UserDao {
3      @Query("SELECT * FROM user")
4      fun getAll(): List<User>
5
6      @Insert
7      fun insertAll(vararg users: User)
8  }
```

Lastly, define your database by extending RoomDatabase:

```
1  @Database(entities = [User::class], version = 1)
2  abstract class AppDatabase : RoomDatabase() {
3      abstract fun userDao(): UserDao
4  }
```

Instantiate your database using Room.databaseBuilder or
Room.inMemoryDatabaseBuilder for a database that persists only in
memory.

SharedPreferences for Lightweight Data Storage

SharedPreferences facilitates the storage of key-value pairs. It's
preferable for storing small amounts of data such as user settings.
Implement SharedPreferences as follows:

```
1  val sharedPref = activity?.getSharedPreferences(
2      getString(R.string.preference_file_key), Context.MODE_PRIVATE)
```

To write data:

```
1  with (sharedPref.edit()) {
2      putInt(getString(R.string.saved_high_score_key), newHighScore)
3      apply()
4  }
```

To retrieve data:

```
1  val highScore = sharedPref.getInt(getString(R.string.
       saved_high_score_key), defaultValue)
```

287

File Handling in Kotlin

For direct file manipulation, Kotlin provides straightforward methods. To write to a file:

```
1   val file = File(context.filesDir, "example.txt")
2   file.writeText("Hello, World!")
```

To read from a file:

```
1   val contents = file.readText()
```

Given that different data persistence methods serve varied purposes in Android development, understanding and implementing them effectively allows for more robust, user-centric applications. Room is ideal for complex data storage and operations, SharedPreferences is suited for preferences and settings, while direct file handling affords granular control over file data.

10.10 Building Dynamic Applications with LiveData and ViewModel

LiveData is an observable data holder class that is lifecycle-aware. It respects the lifecycle of other app components, such as activities, fragments, or services. This means that LiveData will only update component observers that are in an active lifecycle state, such as STARTED or RESUMED.

ViewModel, on the other hand, is designed to store and manage UI-related data in a lifecycle conscious way. The ViewModel allows data to survive configuration changes such as screen rotations. Combining LiveData with ViewModel, Kotlin developers can create robust, manageable, and dynamic Android applications.

Let's delve into the implementation details:

Incorporating ViewModel into Your Application

To use ViewModel, one needs to add the necessary dependency to the build.gradle file of your module:

```
1  dependencies {
2      implementation "androidx.lifecycle:lifecycle-viewmodel-ktx:2.4.0"
3  }
```

After adding the dependency, you can create a class that extends ViewModel. This class will hold the UI-related data that needs to be managed across configuration changes.

```
1  class MyViewModel : ViewModel() {
2      val myLiveData = MutableLiveData<String>()
3  }
```

Here, MyViewModel has a MutableLiveData property named myLiveData. MutableLiveData is a subclass of LiveData that exposes the setValue(T) and postValue(T) methods publicly so you can change the value stored in LiveData. myLiveData is initialized with a type of String.

Using LiveData to Update the UI

To update the UI based on the data in ViewModel, observe the Live-Data within an activity or fragment. You need to call the observe() method, passing the LifecycleOwner and an Observer object. The observer's onChange() method triggers each time the LiveData's data changes, enabling you to update the UI correspondingly.

```
1  class MyActivity : AppCompatActivity() {
2
3      override fun onCreate(savedInstanceState: Bundle?) {
4          super.onCreate(savedInstanceState)
5          setContentView(R.layout.activity_main)
6
7          val model: MyViewModel by viewModels()
8          model.myLiveData.observe(this, Observer<String> { value ->
9              // Update the UI.
10         })
11     }
```

```
12 }
```

In this example, `model.myLiveData.observe()` watches for changes in `myLiveData`. Whenever `myLiveData`'s content changes, it triggers the `Observer`'s onChange method, allowing the UI to be updated with the new data.

Best Practices and Common Patterns

While implementing LiveData and ViewModel, a few best practices can enhance the maintainability and performance of your application:

- Keep the ViewModel free of View components to prevent memory leaks.

- Use a Repository pattern to abstract the data source from View-Model.

- Consider using Data Binding to further minimize the glue code necessary for updating your UI.

- Utilize Transformations.map and Transformations.switchMap for LiveData to perform transformations on the data before it's observed.

Combining LiveData and ViewModel simplifies the development of dynamic Android applications with Kotlin. It helps in managing and updating UI components based on data changes efficiently, ensuring a reactive and seamless user experience.

10.11 Utilizing   Android   Networking Libraries with Kotlin

Networking is an integral part of modern Android applications, allowing apps to communicate with remote servers for data retrieval, submission, and other operations. Kotlin, being a modern language, provides a robust platform to work seamlessly with several networking libraries designed to simplify these operations. In this section, we will discuss the integration and use of popular Android networking libraries in Kotlin, focusing on Retrofit, OkHttp, and Ktor.

Integrating Retrofit for RESTful API Communication

Retrofit is a type-safe HTTP client for Android and Java developed by Square. It turns your HTTP API into a Kotlin interface.

```
1  interface ApiService {
2      @GET("users/{user}/repos")
3      suspend fun listRepos(@Path("user") user: String): List<Repo>
4  }
```

This code snippet defines an interface with Retrofit annotations to describe how HTTP requests will be made. The @GET annotation specifies that this call is a GET request and {user} is replaced with a value passed to the listRepos function. Retrofit works with coroutines, making asynchronous calls concise and straightforward.

To create a Retrofit instance, you need to specify the base URI for the service and configure the converter factory (e.g., Gson for JSON parsing):

```
1  val retrofit = Retrofit.Builder()
2      .baseUrl("https://api.github.com/")
3      .addConverterFactory(GsonConverterFactory.create())
4      .build()
5
6  val apiService = retrofit.create(ApiService::class.java)
```

Errors and responses can be handled using Kotlin's try-catch blocks and Response type:

```
1  try {
2      val response = apiService.listRepos("octocat")
3      if (response.isSuccessful) {
4          // Process data
5      } else {
6          // Handle request error
```

```
7      }
8    } catch (e: Exception) {
9        // Handle unexpected error
10   }
```

OkHttp for Low-Level Networking Tasks

For apps needing fine-grained control over their network operations or those that simply prefer a minimalistic approach, OkHttp provides a powerful yet flexible solution. It can execute calls synchronously with a blocking call or asynchronously using callbacks:

```
1   val client = OkHttpClient()
2   val request = Request.Builder()
3       .url("https://api.github.com/users/octocat/repos")
4       .build()
5
6   client.newCall(request).execute().use { response ->
7       if (!response.isSuccessful) throw IOException("Unexpected code
            $response")
8
9       val responseData = response.body()?.string()
10      // Process response data
11  }
```

Ktor as a Kotlin-first Solution

Ktor is a framework built by JetBrains for creating asynchronous servers and clients in connected systems. It is entirely written in Kotlin and thus provides a more natural syntax when working within Kotlin projects. It supports both client and server-side development, making it a versatile choice for full-stack Kotlin developers. A simple Ktor client request example is as follows:

```
1   val client = HttpClient(CIO) {
2       install(JsonFeature) {
3           serializer = KotlinxSerializer()
4       }
5   }
6   runBlocking {
```

```
7    val response: List<Repo> = client.get("https://api.github.com/users
         /octocat/repos")
8    // Process response
9  }
```

In this configuration, `HttpClient` is set up with the CIO engine and JsonFeature to handle JSON serialization automatically using kotlinx.serialization. The `get` function is a suspending function, making it easy to call within coroutines for asynchronous operations.

Choosing the Right Library for Your Project

The choice of networking library depends on specific project requirements:

- Use Retrofit if you prefer a declarative style for API service definitions and need easy JSON or XML serialization.

- Choose OkHttp for executing custom HTTP requests or when working at a lower level is necessary.

- Opt for Ktor if you are working on a Kotlin-centric project or need coroutine support integrated directly into the client.

Irrespective of the choice, Kotlin's support for these libraries ensures that Android developers can leverage powerful networking capabilities with minimal boilerplate code and maintain a focus on creating feature-rich applications.

10.12 Adding Multimedia and Camera Features

Adding multimedia and camera functionality to an Android application can greatly enhance user engagement and satisfaction. Kotlin offers straightforward and efficient ways to integrate these features, aligning with Android's extensive framework for handling media operations. This section explores the methods to incorporate multimedia playback and camera functionalities into your Kotlin-based Android apps.

Integrating Multimedia Playback

To integrate multimedia playback, such as audio and video, Android provides a MediaPlayer class. This class supports playing both local files and streams from the Internet. Here's a simple example on how to play an audio file from the application's resource directory:

```
1   import android.media.MediaPlayer
2   import androidx.appcompat.app.AppCompatActivity
3   import android.os.Bundle
4
5   class MainActivity : AppCompatActivity() {
6       private lateinit var mediaPlayer: MediaPlayer
7
8       override fun onCreate(savedInstanceState: Bundle?) {
9           super.onCreate(savedInstanceState)
10          setContentView(R.layout.activity_main)
11
12          mediaPlayer = MediaPlayer.create(this, R.raw.sample_audio)
13          mediaPlayer.start() // Start playback
14      }
15
16      override fun onDestroy() {
17          super.onDestroy()
18          mediaPlayer.release() // Release media player resources
19      }
20  }
```

It is important to release the MediaPlayer resources when they are no longer needed to prevent memory leaks and unnecessary resource consumption.

Utilizing the Camera

Adding camera functionality requires more steps, primarily to handle permissions and to integrate with the camera hardware efficiently. Android provides the Camera2 API for accessing and controlling the device's camera hardware.

First, ensure to request the camera permission in your application's AndroidManifest.xml:

```
1  <uses-permission android:name="android.permission.CAMERA" />
```

To use the camera, start by creating a camera capture session. Here is a simplified example to initialize camera capture:

```
1  import android.Manifest
2  import android.content.pm.PackageManager
3  import androidx.appcompat.app.AppCompatActivity
4  import android.os.Bundle
5  import androidx.core.app.ActivityCompat
6  import androidx.core.content.ContextCompat
7
8  class CameraActivity : AppCompatActivity() {
9      // Check if the camera permission is granted
10     private fun isCameraPermissionGranted() =
11         ContextCompat.checkSelfPermission(this, Manifest.permission.
               CAMERA) == PackageManager.PERMISSION_GRANTED
12
13     override fun onCreate(savedInstanceState: Bundle?) {
14         super.onCreate(savedInstanceState)
15         setContentView(R.layout.activity_camera)
16
17         // Request camera permission if not granted
18         if (!isCameraPermissionGranted()) {
19             ActivityCompat.requestPermissions(this, arrayOf(Manifest.
                   permission.CAMERA), 1)
20         }
21     }
22 }
```

Handling the user's response to the permission request and managing the camera to capture photos or videos involves further steps, including configuring camera settings, managing the camera session, and processing the captured images or videos. Due to the complexity and scope of camera API usage, developers should refer to the official Android documentation for detailed guidelines and best practices.

Concluding Remarks

Adding multimedia and camera features can significantly enrich the functionality and appeal of Android applications. While the MediaPlayer class provides a straightforward method for integrating audio and video playback, the Camera2 API offers comprehensive control over the device's camera, though with increased complexity. Proper handling of resources and permissions is crucial to ensure a seamless user experience and operational efficiency. It is recommended to explore Android's official guides and sample codes to fully master these capabilities.

10.13   Publishing Your Android App

Publishing your Android application is the final step in the journey of application development. This process involves several crucial steps to ensure that your app is ready for the public and adheres to the guidelines set by the Google Play Store. The following sections will guide you through preparing your application for release, configuring the app's listing, and finally, submitting it to the Google Play Store.

To begin, it is essential to prepare your application for release. This involves ensuring that your code is free of bugs, that all app functionalities are working as intended, and that your app meets all the requirements specified by Google Play. Additionally, you need to generate a signed APK or Android App Bundle (AAB) file, which is a requirement for uploading your app to the Play Store. The signing process involves using a private key to certify that you are the developer of the app. This can be accomplished using the following command in the Android Studio terminal:

```
1  ./gradlew bundleRelease
```

This command generates an AAB file located in <project>/build/outputs/bundle/release/ directory. It is critical to keep your keystore and private key secure, as they are necessary for future updates to your application.

Before uploading the app, you need to create a listing on Google Play Store. This involves providing detailed information about your app, including its title, description, and screenshots. The description should be concise and highlight the key features of your app to attract potential users. Create a compelling set of screenshots that showcase the functionality and design of your app, as these are often the first elements that potential users will see. Additionally, you must select a content rating, set a privacy policy, and decide on a pricing model for your app.

Once the listing is configured, you can proceed to upload the AAB file to Google Play. Navigate to the 'Release Management' section in the Google Play Console, and select 'App Releases'. Here you can upload your AAB file and fill in the release information. Google Play Console provides instructions for creating a release, which includes specifying the version code and release notes. The release notes are important as they inform users about new features, bug fixes, or improvements in the current release.

After uploading and saving your release, the final step is to submit it for review. Google will review your app to ensure it complies with their policies and guidelines. This review process can take several days. Once approved, your app will be published on Google Play Store and become available to users worldwide.

In summary, publishing an Android app involves preparing your application for release, creating a compelling app listing, uploading your app, and submitting it for review. By following these steps carefully, you can ensure a smooth submission process and increase the likelihood of your application's success on the Google Play Store.

www.ingramcontent.com/pod-product-compliance
Lightning Source LLC
LaVergne TN
LVHW052057060326
832903LV00061B/3087